HUNTING, FISHING, AND ENVIRONMENTAL VIRTUE

Reconnecting Sportsmanship and Conservation

HUNTING, FISHING, AND ENVIRONMENTAL VIRTUE

Reconnecting Sportsmanship and Conservation

Charles J. List

Oregon State University Press, Corvallis

APR 2014

The paper in this book meets the guidelines for permanence
and durability of the Committee on Production Guidelines
for Book Longevity of the Council on Library Resources
and the minimum requirements of the American National
Standard for Permanence of Paper for Printed Library
Materials Z39.48-1984.

Library of Congress Cataloging-in-Publication Data

List, Charles J. (Charles James)
Hunting, fishing, and environmental virtue : reconnecting
sportsmanship and conservation / Charles J. List.
       pages cm
Includes bibliographical references and index.
ISBN 978-0-87071-714-7 (alkaline paper) --
ISBN 978-0-87071-715-4 (e-book)
1. Hunting--Philosophy. 2. Fishing--Philosophy. 3.
Hunting--Moral and ethical aspects. 4. Fishing--Moral
and ethical aspects. 5. Environmental ethics. 6. Nature
conservation--Philosophy. I. Title.
  SK14.3.L57 2013
  639'.1--dc23
                                     2012044624

OSU
Oregon State
UNIVERSITY

Oregon State University Press
121 The Valley Library
Corvallis OR 97331-4501
541-737-3166 • fax 541-737-3170
http://osupress.oregonstate.edu

CONTENTS

ACKNOWLEDGMENTS

Thanks first to my friend and fellow angler/philosopher John Spissinger, who challenged me to think about leisure and who read and commented on many versions of this book. Without his support and enthusiasm for this project, it may never have been completed.

Thanks also to my wife and colleague, Beth Dixon, for her careful comments on earlier drafts and constant support.

For permission to use portions of articles I've published, thanks to the editors of *Environmental Ethics* and *Ethics & the Environment*.

SUNY-Plattsburgh graciously granted me a sabbatical leave during which much of the writing was done.

Students in my environmental ethics classes have listened to these ideas and have responded in their usual good natured and positive way. I thank them for their forbearance.

Thanks finally to two excellent readers for Oregon State University Press, Nathan Kowalsky and Michael Nelson, whose comments made the arguments much sharper.

This book is dedicated to the memory of my grandmother, Anne List, who fished until she was one hundred.

INTRODUCTION

Aldo Leopold once declared that North American hunters are puzzled. Seven decades later, I'd say that not much has changed. If anything, things have gotten worse. Hunting and angling have lost their ethical center. We seem incapable of rationally defending them against moral critics and, equally importantly, against pretended friends in commerce and politics. Defenders of field sports have been reduced to appeals to economic activity generated, car accidents avoided, and giving "fair chase."

There was a time over a hundred years ago when hunters and anglers would proudly point to the power of field sports to instill the character of the "Sportsman." As Teddy Roosevelt saw it, field sports cultivate a "vigorous manliness" with its attendant virtues of hardiness, self-reliance, and resolution. Since Roosevelt's image of the sportsman is clearly outdated, I will argue for a revised thesis, one with a distinctly environmental flavor. My purpose in this book is to refine and refocus a virtue-based defense of field sports by connecting particular environmental virtues with the activities. The "sportsman thesis," as I shall call it, holds that field sports develop character. By teaching young people to hunt and fish, and by guiding them through the process, certain character traits may be established in them. These character traits are confirmed and deepened by continual practice.

As an avid hunter and angler, I fervently desire that the sportsman thesis is sound. But as a philosopher, I have deep suspicions. On the one hand, it just seems right to me that my commitment to conservation issues and, more broadly, environmental causes is due to my participation in field sports. On the other hand, my philosophical side wants to know how it is even possible that participation in an activity can, even partially, form character. What kind of character is formed? Why are some hunters and anglers conservationists and others not? Are there other ways besides field sports to develop such a character?

If the sportsman thesis is to be revived, these questions will need answers. The list of character traits will need to be revised. The character developed by field sports will need to be updated from the archaic making of a virile and manly wilderness hunter to the making of an environmentalist.

To effect this critical evaluation and transformation of the sportsman thesis, I first consider in Part One some views about the nature of those activities that seem capable of virtue-building and character modification.

This investigation will lead us to look at the nature of skills and expertise, the development of practical reason, and the role of leisure activities in the development of virtue. Once we've discovered that field sports as activities are at least capable of developing character, I look, in Part Two, at the kind of character they might develop. Aldo Leopold's work provides the basic guidelines for this revised conception of character.

Field sports are morally suspect. I am fully aware of the literature devoted to deepening and continuing this suspicion. I will not offer a direct refutation of the views of animal rights theorists because that would be a different book. I will, in Part Three, carefully consider several core arguments that have found their way into almost every critical assessment of field sports. Once these arguments are successfully answered, it will still be open for critics to maintain that animals have rights and interests that we should not violate in field sports. But I will at least establish that there is an ethically sound alternative. This virtue-ethics approach has deep historical roots, the philosophical sophistication to answer objections, and the power to make far-reaching suggestions for the future of field sports.

The task in Part Four is to influence the future direction of field sports such that they retain contact with the enlivened sportsman thesis. I will make practical suggestions to sportsmen and critically examine some entrenched countervailing policies, institutions, and cultural assumptions. Governmental natural resource agencies are driven to supply an artificial abundance of game and then cast field sports as tools of scientific wildlife management. Commercial interests in equipment sales, destination hunting and angling, money tournaments, and television revenues are also threats to the ability of field sports to generate environmental virtues. Outdoor education needs to be reoriented by the sportsman thesis. Practices of hunters and anglers regarding "varmints" and "trash fish," stocking, and catch-and-release fishing need critical examination. Finally, alternative forms of outdoor recreation need to be examined in light of the sportsman thesis.

The sportsman thesis in its revised environmental form offers the best ethical justification of field sports. But its acceptance will require deep changes in both the behavior of sportsmen and in the institutions that purport to support field sports.

A more detailed chapter outline will help supplement this introduction.

Chapter One explains and critically evaluates several historically important versions of the sportsman thesis and makes the case that it was primarily a hypothesis that catered to the education of young gentlemen. I identify several central problems faced by any defense of this thesis. Chapter Two addresses one of the philosophical problems identified in the critical evaluation: is it really possible for activities to generate virtues as the sportsman thesis assumes? What can the concept of expertise tell us about this process? In Chapter Three, I will discuss how it is that activities might actually generate virtue. That is, once we know what kinds of activities are capable of generating virtue, we need to know how this process actually works.

These three chapters, forming Part One, are meant to supply the necessary philosophical background prior to a defense of field sports as potential engines of virtue.

In Chapter Four, I consider the historical evolution of the thesis from its original form to a later conception of sportsman as conservationist. This move, though it is in the right direction, is inadequate because conservation is a necessity for others, such as farmers and loggers, not engaged in field sports. Rather, as Aldo Leopold realized, if the sportsman thesis is truly to be saved, the virtues acquired by participants in field sports must be available to a wider range of outdoor activities and these activities must require an ethic that goes beyond what is economically expedient and requires more than merely voting right and giving some money to conservation organizations (to paraphrase Leopold). In Chapter Five I argue that if the sportsman thesis is to be revitalized, participants in field sports must measure their activity against the good of the biotic community. This newly articulated good will explain the list of environmental virtues inherent in field sports developed in Chapter Six.

Before this updated sportsman/environmentalist thesis can be accepted, several powerful objections must be answered in Part Three. One objection is this: granting that field sports generate environmental virtue, but recognizing that other activities such as gardening or wildlife photography do as well, why not substitute one of those non-lethal outdoor activities? Nothing will be lost—if the same virtues are generated— and animals will not be killed. To answer this objection, in Chapter Seven, I will develop a means for distinguishing among several outdoor activities in terms of goods sought in addition to the virtues developed. These goods include the food provided by the animal acquired and the aesthetic experiences of the participants in the activity. Second, when critics attack field sports they focus almost exclusively on "sport" hunting and fishing as opposed to "subsistence" or "commercial." The reasoning seems obvious: participants in field sports don't have to hunt, killing animals for sport is wrong, so field sports are wrong. The answer to this objection requires a reexamination of the category of "sport" as applied to hunting and fishing in Chapter Eight. A third important objection is that the updated version of the sportsman thesis that I articulate is no more than an ethical "code" followed by some hunters and anglers who perceive themselves as being gentlemen. This is just self-deception and camouflage according to these critics. It helps hunters and anglers mask what they are really doing: murdering innocent animals. No "code following" is sufficient to make this activity moral. This objection will be considered in Chapter Nine.

These objections are central to the general animal rights and welfare critique of field sports. But to successfully answer them is not to refute the animal-welfare worldview. I don't think that is possible because that view has all the hallmarks of religious belief. What I can do is offer an alternative that grounds field sports in a well-established ethical view, one capable of making sense of its activities and providing much-needed guidance for its practitioners.

Once these objections are answered the way is cleared to consider some current and future issues in field sports. In Part Four, I will take up these issues. In Chapter Ten, I consider the civic value of field sports. How should sportsmen place their activities in the civic virtues demanded by society in general? In Chapter Eleven, issues related to the ever-increasing commercialization of field sports, both in terms of equipment and competitions, are considered. Chapter Twelve discusses outdoor education and hunter education, which have real impact on both hunters and anglers. How should these programs be revised to account for the sportsman thesis? In Chapter Thirteen, I take up a number of issues concerning game management, including stocking, catch-and-release fishing, and policies dealing with "varmints" and other "unwelcome" animals. Chapter Fourteen discusses the relationship of field sports to other outdoor activities. The goal is to enlist like activities in the pursuit of environmental virtues, and also provide a reasonable way of resolving cases of conflict between sportsmen and other outdoor enthusiasts.

Part One
Philosophy and Field Sports

In this first part I discuss the history and philosophical background for the sportsman thesis. Classically, there was thought to be a close connection between skills and virtues, one that has received considerable attention recently. After a brief tour of the history of the sportsman thesis, I consider three ways in which the development of skills has been connected to the development of virtue: practical reasoning, mentorship, and leisure.

Chapter One: The Sportsman Thesis

The sportsman thesis, broadly speaking, holds that hunting and angling are instrumental in the development of character. It's a thesis as old as ancient Greece and as new as the latest issue of *Fly Rod & Reel*. Its career is full of twists and turns, rejection and rediscovery. While I shall sample this history in order to establish the pedigree of the thesis, I am really more interested in the philosophical issues and doubts about it. I believe this thesis, after clarification and argument, will provide the basis for a much-needed ethical foundation for hunting and field sports in general. Since, historically, the thesis has been directed at the education of young people, we should look first at its history in this context.

The Historical Role of the Sportsman Thesis

This sportsman thesis has a long and distinguished career. One version of the thesis was endorsed by Plato. In the Laws, we see that he recommends only a certain kind of hunting as a worthy pursuit for the education of young men or "athletes" of his envisioned ideal society. For Plato, the preeminent virtue to be cultivated by an education in hunting is courage, because these hunters are being trained for war.[1]

> . . . *the best variety, is the chase of a four-footed quarry in reliance upon one's horse, one's dogs, and one's own limbs, where the hunters—those, that is, who cultivate godlike courage—all hunt in their own persons and achieve all their success by running, striking, and shooting.*[2]

Plato thinks that the virtue of courage is both extremely important, hence "godlike," and that only a certain kind of hunting is a way of inculcating it. There are several things of interest for us in this quote. The education for the virtue of courage needs to be carefully considered. Few would argue that courage in general is a bad thing, but some will definitely argue that training young people for war is a bad thing. A second insight available from Plato is that what he has in mind is a certain style of hunting as primarily responsible for virtue development: a sort of mad dashing around on horseback (with no stirrups), chasing dogs that are tracking rabbits or other four-legged game. This activity is of course comparable to contemporary fox hunting. It does seem to habituate some of the skills one might need to fight the kind of war prevalent in classical Greece and insofar as one has these skills, courage is demonstrated by merely exercising them on the battlefield. Problematic as it is, this idea of hunting as training for courage and war is recapitulated in American lore about the soldier/woodsmen of the Revolutionary War.[3]

A different assessment of the educational powers of hunting and fishing is found in Izaak Walton's seventeenth century book The Compleat Angler. This dialogue, in which Piscator the angler teaches his art to Venator the hunter, begins with each of them arguing in favor of their chosen recreations. (There is also another character in the discussion, a falconer.)

Many of the arguments rehearsed by Walton's Piscator for the virtues of angling over hunting are downright silly. These include references to the mythological importance of water in Christian theology, the fishy occupations of Christ's disciples, and the curative powers of healing spas. Philosophically, the issue is discussed in terms of the relative merits of a more "contemplative recreation" like angling over a more active one like hunting. We must imagine Walton's angler wandering placidly along a quiet stream as opposed to the hunter charging around on a horse yelling at the top of his lungs. As Walton says: there are arguments for each of these approaches, but "both these meet together, and do most properly belong to the most honest, ingenuous, quiet, and harmless art of Angling."[4] While it appears that hunting, for Walton, is too much devoted to "action," angling contains a proper measure of contemplation as well. Indeed, from what Walton says after this, it appears that angling is primarily recommended because it contains a large share of contemplation. He discusses various anglers he has known or read and extols their "Godlike" contemplative states, whether they are clergy or layman. This contrast is captured in these verses of this old angler's song:

> Sports of mighty Nimrod's chusing, All your mischiefs I will shun;
> Broken bones and grievous bruising, Glorious scars by Hunters won.
> Come, then harmless recreation, Holding out the Angler's Reed;
> Nurse of pleasing Contemplation, By the stream thy wand'rings lead . . .

The measure presented by these verses, and by Walton, is that of "pleasing contemplation" over "grievous bruising" and "broken bones." As these lines indicate, there was a concern for human health as well as happiness in the comparison of angling with hunting. The latter offers us action at the risk of bodily damage; the former harmless recreation together with contemplation.

Plato and Walton present an interesting contrast regarding the kinds of virtues one might expect to achieve in hunting as opposed to angling. The historical evidence that hunting and angling were thought to have the capacity to generate virtue at the same time reinforces the educational power of these activities. Of course, it remains to be seen that they do have this power. For our purposes it is sufficient at this point to note that at least some virtues (courage or contemplation) are said to be inculcated by these activities.

I shall in what follows treat hunting and angling together as field sports that are capable of forming one's character. Plato and Walton seem to disagree about the exact nature of this character in that Plato is promoting hunting for courage and Walton angling for contemplation. They do agree, however, that the activities are capable of generating virtue, and so endorse the educational value of field sports for character development. As we'll see in the next section, these differences are erased in the Americanized version of the sportsman thesis. Fundamentally, fishing is just one kind of hunting where the implements and quarry are different but the skills required are the same. Ethically, as virtue-generating activities, they stand or fall together. It is interesting that Plato makes this same point when he is illustrating his logical "method of division." He rapidly takes his followers through a series of logical divisions wherein hunting is an "art of acquisition" and angling is a kind of hunting wherein the animals sought are water animals and the technique used is that of spearing them from below by drawing an "angle" or a hook up from beneath them to catch them. We shall have reason to return to this idea when a definition of hunting becomes necessary.

What unites hunting and fishing as activities of character formation are the basic skills shared and ultimately the virtues generated. Contrary to Plato and Walton, I will argue that the virtues generated are the same.

The Pastimes of Stream and Woodland

A mid-nineteenth-century version of the sportsman thesis is directed at American hunters and anglers with aristocratic leanings:

> The pastimes of stream and woodland . . . are the characteristic
> exercises of many of the noblest properties of man's nature . . . they
> call into exertion courage, perseverance, sagacity, strength, activity,

> [and] caution . . . they are the wholesome machinery of excitement;
> of hope and fear, and joy and sorrow, regret and rejoicing; they
> are at once the appetite and the food of manhood. . . . Instead of
> being antagonist[ic] meanings, the sportsman and the gentleman are
> [becoming] . . . synonymous terms.[5]

The claim that field sports will inculcate those very virtues required for one to become a sportsman and a gentleman is so old fashioned yet, somehow, so attractive. Even though the goal of becoming a gentleman may have faded, the other "synonymous" goal of being a "sportsman" has remained viable for many years.[6] For instance, in *Today's Hunter*, a guide for hunter education classes, "the sportsman" is the ultimate stage of hunter development following the other four earlier and more childish or adolescent stages: shooting the firearm, limiting out or getting the most animals legally allowed, acquiring trophies, and finally, a focus on the method used—firearm or bow, bait or fly rod. The sportsman stage is described as follows: "Success is measured by the total experience—the appreciation of the out-of-doors and the animal being hunted, the process of the hunt, and the companionship of other hunters."[7] This characterization of the sportsman implies that field sports are a way to move through certain stages to the ultimate mastery of essential skills with the goal of the acquisition and cultivation of certain qualities of character. In the older version, facing a grizzly bear requires courage and hooking a salmon requires perseverance. These are important and widely recognized virtues. To become a sportsman is to have these virtues as parts of one's character available for exercise in all walks of life. An activity that allows one to exercise the emotions—of hope and fear, joy and sorrow at the right time and in the right way—is a valuable educational tool.

That old wilderness hunter, Teddy Roosevelt, famously sought to establish the thesis and bring about the environmental conditions necessary for Americans to continue to benefit from such qualities of character. No longer is the goal of becoming a gentleman foremost. It is now the "wilderness hunter" Roosevelt envisions who will attain certain virtues.

> The wilderness hunter must not only show skill in the use of
> the rifle and address in finding and approaching game, but he must
> also show the qualities of hardihood, self-reliance, and resolution
> needed for effectively grappling with his wild surroundings.[8]

The sportsman thesis, as I will define it, is less specific than these two samples. I shall discuss the sportsman thesis as the claim that field sports are capable of inculcating a set of virtues that collectively determine the character of the sportsman. I shall not specify yet the exact set of virtues thus inculcated, because, as we've seen, this list is subject to some variation.

Problems for the Sportsman Thesis

There are serious immediate challenges to the truth and viability of the sportsman thesis. Perhaps, one might argue, there's good reason for current suspicions. The first philosophical problem is the gap between teaching a "technical" activity and moral education. David Roochnik raises the classical problem for Plato's belief about hunting leading to courage: "Can a specifically technical subject have a beneficial moral effect on the student?"[9] This question is debated at length in Plato's early dialogues and the outcome remains controversial. The central problem, as Roochnik notes, is "a gap between a technical and a moral education."[10] This gap is exposed by the cases of the students who are taught a technical skill such as hunting but fail to become morally excellent. On the other hand, for those students who do achieve moral excellence after training, it could be argued that they may have already had it before the training. This problem will provide focus for much of what follows in this part.

This is made all the more urgent when some argue that field sports, far from producing a good character, actually do the opposite. After all, if hunting and angling can lead to virtue, they can also lead to vice. A fair statement of this view was given by Dr. Benjamin Rush in 1790, at a point in history when hunting was, as it is in the present, less than popular. He states that hunting, far from inculcating various virtues of the gentleman, rather is responsible for the development of many vices. Included in his list are these: hunting "hardens the heart," it "creates habits of idleness," it leads men to "low, bad company," it leads to intemperance in both eating and alcohol consumption, and finally it is unhealthy from the point of view of exposure to fevers and accident. This is all added to the general charge of cruelty of hunting animals.[11] The problem presented is that for every example of virtue we might attempt to derive from hunting and angling, someone might reasonably derive a vice.

Another obvious problem for the sportsman thesis is its elitist and exclusionary nature, and this comes in several forms. First, feminists and progressives will find the exclusionary sexism and classism of the thesis unacceptable. Indeed the very term "sportsman" seems exclusionary. Looking back to its popularity in this country in the late nineteenth century, we can see that the books and articles were primarily addressed to male readers with aristocratic pretensions. Teddy Roosevelt says: "The chase is among the best of all national pastimes; it cultivates that vigorous manliness for the lack of which in a nation, as in an individual, the possession of no other qualities can possibly atone."[12] His intended audience is clear.[13]

Also excluded in this early version of the thesis are those hunters and anglers who hunted "for the table" or "pot hunters," as well as market hunters who primarily sold their captured and killed animals to food and clothing markets. The differences between the sportsman and the pot or market hunters often amounted to class and ethnic distinctions. Those who had to hunt or fish or who materially benefited from such, so the thinking went, couldn't possibly obtain the spiritual and ethical goods available to sportsman. Those who identified themselves as sportsmen also objected to the crass techniques used to capture animals by these excluded groups, for example nets and punt guns (a kind of shrapnel cannon) being two of the greatest offenders. The use of these "mechanized" forms of hunting and angling threatened to completely wipe out many species of game and non-game animals.

A third exclusionary use of the thesis turns the critical standards inward and sets up a style for all sportsmen to follow. Codes and standards were published allowing one to judge one's own standing as well as that of others hoping to attain the status of being a "true sportsman." There was then, as now, a complex vocabulary to learn, a way to dress, and a way to act. The contrast was often made between these highly cultivated hunters and anglers and those who, for one reason or another, were unable to understand or achieve the moral perfection of the sportsman.

Conclusion

The idea that virtues might be derived from field sports is one with a rich history. The question I wish to pursue is whether there is anything that can be salvaged from this thesis, given the manifest problems it faces both philosophically and socially. The gap between practice and virtue and the various historical exclusions are not the only problems for the sportsman thesis. But, of immediate concern is bridging the gap between field sports and character development. To do so we'll begin with the concept of expertise.

Chapter Two: From Beginner to Expert

It is difficult to see how a good character may be derived from doing field sports because we don't yet know how activities in general might even promote the development of virtue. It's like someone saying that a given food is good for you, but not telling you what it is about the food that makes it so. What is it about certain activities that might make them good for you? Are hunting and angling the right sort of activities to inculcate virtue? If the sportsman thesis is meant to be a hypothesis about the education of youth, then we would predict that teaching young people to hunt and fish will lead eventually to the development of certain virtues collected under the label of "sportsmen." We can better understand this thesis, endorsed by philosophers, clerics, and politicians, if we look at its philosophical presuppositions.

Classically, education for virtue presupposed a certain overall goal or end which the virtues developed would serve. So, for instance, if the goal is happiness, as Aristotle asserts, then the list of virtues he identifies is to be justified by serving this goal. Plato's goal of a stable ideal state is served by the virtues he identifies. The educational question is how best to inculcate those desirable virtues which serve the chosen end; which activities are most appropriate? But if certain activities are to be the means for developing virtues, we must answer some prior questions.

First, what is it about the nature of activities themselves that makes it plausible to think that they might be even *capable* of generating virtue? Second, what motives must participants bring to the activity in order that virtues are generated? The first question will inform this chapter and the second one the next. Only when we've satisfied ourselves on these points can we finally go on to ask, in Part Two, what specific list of virtues might be aimed at.

The argument I will give in this chapter is roughly this: the goal of expertise and mastery of an activity is at least partially a matter of skill development. Becoming an expert in an activity is determined by meeting public and historically justified standards of skillfulness. Achieving expertise will be philosophically explained by the development of "practical reason." This capacity is refined by practice under the supervision of quality instruction and mentoring in the face of difficult circumstances. Thus, those activities best suited to enable virtues are those that require practical reason at its highest level. And, as we shall see, practical reason is a highly adaptable and thus useful capacity.

Field Sport Expertise

Since the sportsman thesis is an educational hypothesis, we might look at what it takes to move from the first steps in learning an activity to becoming an expert in it. This process, we shall see, is closely connected to character development. The topic of expertise is very broad and only certain parts will be highlighted here.[1]

Learning to hunt for land animals is different from learning to hunt for fish in several obvious ways. But historically they involve the same set of skills. In both cases, one must know how to find animals of the right sort and know how to get close to them.[2] Learning these skills, along with the more signal ones of shooting or casting, is the educational process for hunting and angling. This kind of education is very different from the kind of book learning in the school classroom or in front of the computer screen. In field sports students learn how to *do* something.[3] We come to know *how* in addition to knowing *that*. The expert in field sports will have no difficulty *demonstrating* to students how to do something but may find it nearly impossible to *describe* in words that same process. Experts in these areas teach by hands-on guidance and example. It is simply impossible to teach someone to cast a fly line by description. It must be shown and then practiced. So expertise in these sorts of activities is nurtured by practice under the careful observation of a willing teacher. Such teachers, ideally, will be the repositories of the highest standards of skillfulness.[4] Such teaching does not fit the typical classroom model as a cognitive transference of knowledge, where the teacher speaks and the student listens and remembers. This feature, we shall see, is very important for bridging the gap between character development and activities.[5]

What we need is a philosophically suggestive description of this alternative learning process. Others have already done much of this, especially where the skills in question are of a more cognitive nature. Skills such as mathematical calculation and chess playing, puzzle solving and even navigation are frequently used to illustrate the need for practice and its connection to virtue development.[6] But we shall need to understand this connection in areas of more physical skillfulness.

Practical Reason as a Bridge

Practical reasoning results in performing the best action in the circumstances to achieve a goal, something experts seem to do effortlessly. An expert angler ties on a particular fly and begins to catch fish; a hunter works the dog down though a swamp as opposed to up over a higher ridge. These are routine results of practical reason; not bits of reasoning concluding with a belief in the truth of some proposition, but rather they conclude in an action that may or may not succeed.

Practical reasoning or *phronesis* is prudential thinking: a combination of knowing what to do and having the requisite skill to do it.[7] Practical reasoning is more than knowing some general rules, principles, or background knowledge that may aid in the decisions one must make, even though it does require this. To conclude that it is going to rain tomorrow, based upon the forecast is very different from deciding what one will do when fishing in the rain. Smoothly doing *now* what needs to be done is a result of long hours of practice or what educators call habituation. When beginning anglers want to know *why* a leader is tied the way it is, the teacher should be ready with an appeal to background information about fly-line behavior, tippet strength, and hook size. But the question of which leader to actually use in these particular circumstances is answered by practical reason taking account of current conditions. The background knowledge about field sports fills thousands of volumes in libraries. "How to fish" and "how to hunt" books promise a lifetime of reading. This background knowledge contributes to, but is not itself practical reason.

Besides background knowledge, the expert will have access to years of experience in similar situations. The more experience and practice one has in fishing trout or hunting grouse, the better one's chances of success in solving the problems one faces. Practical reasoning to solve a current problem by performing the right action may depend on both general background knowledge and experience. But it is different from each in that it is a doing. As such it requires two stages: diagnosis, often by use of background knowledge, and problem solving by use of experience and skill.[8] That is, we need to be able to correctly ascertain the salient or relevant features of the situation we are in, whether we are solving a problem in navigation or medicine, hunting or angling, before we can act to solve the problem we face. In hunting and angling, we need to be able to diagnose what the problem is before we solve it. In some cases there is a conscious separation of diagnosis from problem solution, as in medicine. In other cases they form a continuous line.

Hunting and angling, looked at from this point of view, are a series of problems one is trying to solve in the face of incomplete knowledge and rapidly changing conditions. When people are beginning to learn to hunt or fish, one tends to teach them some general rules or principles they can follow. For example, in teaching a beginner to fly fish one might say to "match the hatch" which means to use a fly that matches in size, color, and profile those insects hatching at that time. This is a good rule and one that will produce fish. But as one becomes more experienced this rule will be frequently violated if the situation calls for it. One might go up in hook size or use a contrasting fly. It all depends on the circumstances or the salient features of the situation. Maybe nothing is hatching. Becoming an expert means knowing when to violate the rules. For example, there is a fly-fishing technique called "Czech-style nymphing." One proponent of this method says:

> . . . it would be wrong to imply that the top practitioners of this method apply it like automatons. Skillfully reading the water to identify high-value targets, then covering them thoroughly, is the way to their consistent success.[9]

The elements of diagnosis, "reading the water," and action, "covering them thoroughly," are clearly evident here.

"Reading the water"—having a sense for where fish are likely to be—is an excellent example of practical reasoning diagnosis at a very high level. The problem of finding fish requires diagnostic abilities that include but are not limited to: knowledge of the ways water moves around rocks, knowledge of currents both at the surface and bottom, water clarity, the effect of shadow and light on water, water temperature in relation to depth. These will provide partial answers to the question: why did you cast that fly there? But equally important in answering this question are the current salient features, awareness of which derives from experience and habit. One is tempted to say that one casts that fly right there because it is what one has always done in these circumstances. Practical reasoning draws upon these twin forces of experience and background knowledge for solutions to specific problems.

Reading natural signs in hunting and angling is the diagnostic ability to reason to the best explanation. For example, one needs to be able to read various "rise forms" when fishing for trout. When fish rise, they may do it in a splashy, excited way, even jumping out of the water on occasion, or they may rise more sedately and quietly. There are innumerable in-between cases as well. The trout angler needs to be able to read these natural signs for what they are: signs of what insects are being targeted by the fish. In hunting, there are many analogies to this, but one that comes to mind might be called "reading the dog." Here the sign is less closely connected to the cause: whereas the fish actually makes the rise form, the dog by its behavior is indirectly giving the hunter a sign as to where a bird might be. How staunch is the dog? Is the tail moving? Which direction is the dog pointing given the wind direction? The diagnostic reading of natural signs is more difficult here because the signs are further removed from their causes.

The various skills habituated by fly fishing—fly tying, knot tying, casting, reading the water, wading, for example—cannot be separated from the whole. They are strands in the fabric. Expertise is the quality of the whole cloth. The expert has access to thorough background knowledge, stores of experience, and the habits or skills of rapid diagnosis and the dexterity to solve the problem. Practical reason is displayed in expertise. What is more important for the sportsman thesis, as we will see, is that practical reason is also required for virtue and character formation. It promises to bridge the gap between activities and virtues by providing the template for both solving practical problems and equally solving ethical or environmental problems. As we shall see, ethical problems arising in field sports engage practical reason just as do those concerning reading the water or the covert.

Mentoring

Becoming an expert hunter or angler requires a highly developed practical reason. How does the beginner come to eventually achieve this? Well, the answer is obviously by practicing. It takes hours and hours of practice to develop the skill of dead drifting a nymph to "cover the water" adequately. But this is never enough. One actually needs teachers to help in this process. A student with due diligence might make some progress without the benefit of a teacher, as when one watches someone fish from afar and is able pick up on the technique being employed. But that is the exception. More often someone needs to step forward as an instructor and mentor. Indeed every student wishing to achieve excellence in hunting and angling will look for every opportunity to learn from an expert. The relation between expert and novice is of particular importance when we realize the role of standards for achievement. The teacher embodies the standards of performance sought by the student. These standards not only define the shape of a perfect cast but also the character of the sportsman.

The role of mentors is absolutely central to the eventual virtue development of students.[10] They reinforce the bridge between activities and character education by redirecting practical reason in their students toward features of *ethical* salience, as they concurrently point to more practical features.

These standards of behavior and excellence in performance are parts of the traditions of hunting and angling. The specific character sought in the sportsman thesis evolves as the traditions evolve. For Plato it was courage, for Walton contemplation, for sportsmen of the nineteenth century is was being a gentleman. And as we'll see, the tradition has evolved yet again so that being a conservationist has become a standard. These standards of behavior are mirrored in the standards of performance emulated by the student. As hunting and angling technology evolves, so too must the standards of excellence governing behavior. The traditions of hunting and angling provide the context and rationale for the expert teacher's advice and admonitions.

Stochastic Arts

Another reason activities like field sports need good mentoring is that the salient features for students are at times exceptionally subtle. As a result, sometimes the abilities of experts seem almost magical and inexplicable. When my fishing partner lifts his line after drifting a nymph and there is a trout on the hook, it seems impossible that he would know that it is there. He'll say he thought he saw a slight hesitation in the leader as it drifted by. These "educated guesses" or hunches are as prevalent as black flies in the spring. What role do they have in helping us to understand expertise?

The causal factors involved in stochastic arts are so complex and multiple as to make choices appear random or at best mere hunches.[11] One example of such an art might be weather prediction. Another, as Matthew Crawford in his book *Shop Class as Soul Craft* argues, is engine repair and other shop class subjects.

> . . . *some diagnostic situations contain so many variables, and symptoms can be so under-determining of causes, that explicit analytical reasoning comes up short. What is required then is the kind of judgment that arises only from experience; hunches rather than rules.*[12]

One reason hunters and anglers often "come up short," or, in the phrase more often heard in this context, "get skunked," is that the list of variables is long and daunting. Variables such as time of year, temperature, wind direction, and hatches are involved as well as many others. Hunting depends on not only the analytical powers and physical skills of hunters but also these other factors, which because they are so numerous and changeable, often get classified as "luck" or as Aristotle said, the "benefits of fate." In field sports the concept of luck is built into the very fabric of the practices. A general greeting on the stream or in the woods is "having any luck?" This explains the central role in field sports by factors that are not under the control of hunters and anglers. Indeed, there are various rituals hunters and anglers might perform to minimize the role played by luck.[13] As Crawford says, experience helps one to pay more attention to those hunches that might reduce the frequency of failure, but the control is never absolute because the causal factors are simply innumerable. For the beginner, these causal factors become salient under the guidance of mentors. Only in canned hunts or stocked fishing ponds is one guaranteed results, and the reason these are rejected as actual cases of hunting and angling is that the element of contingency has been eliminated: "shooting fish in a barrel" is neither hunting nor angling.

Conclusion

The sportsman thesis is best understood as an educational hypothesis. The concept of expertise helps us to understand this thesis in several ways. First, hunting and angling are activities of practical reason, requiring both background knowledge and experience united by diagnosis and practice to solve problems skillfully. This is the way the best action is arrived at based on one's diagnostic skills and one's ability to carry out the planned action. To catch a trout I must diagnose where it is likely to be, what it is likely to eat, and have the skills necessary to put the right fly in the right spot at the right time. These are the features salient to this situation. Mastering these skills is what it is to be an expert in this area. Second, expertise is embodied in mentors who model both the technical excellence and the ethical behavior of the sportsman. Finally, expertise is continually challenged by the stochastic nature of these enterprises: action in the face of uncertainty, hunches rather than reasons. This is made all the more challenging by the huge number of variables one must account for sometimes by hunches and guesses. In the face of these difficulties, having expert teachers and mentors to guide one becomes crucial.

Practical reasoning is necessary for both expertise in practical arts and ethical decision making. But it is not sufficient with regard to character formation because participants must choose these activities in the right spirit. What is it about these activities that motivate participants to seek excellence both technically and ethically?

Chapter Three: Choosing Character-Enriching Activities

While it may be clearer now what it means to be an expert at hunting or fishing, and how difficult it is to achieve practical wisdom in these areas, little has been said about character and how these activities might develop it as declared in the sportsman thesis. What is it about certain activities that make them a particularly suitable choice for character education? I shall argue that leisure activities, suitably defined, are connected with the life of enhancing one's excellence by offering the prospect of character development. The pursuit of excellence is the pursuit of virtue, and one's virtues are collectively called one's character. Thus, together with mentoring for practical reason, the choice to pursue virtue bridges the gap between technical activities and morality.

Because both virtue development and skill development rely on practice, there is good reason for thinking that virtues are related to skills.[1] Virtues are certainly developed in the same *way* one develops skills, that is by forming habits based on practice and guidance. So, the thinking is that, if we want students to be good at playing the piano we will have them practice, and if we want young people to be courageous we have them practice that too. It is unfortunate that the term "virtue" currently is almost synonymous with *moral* virtue. When philosophers introduce "virtue ethics" as a moral theory, they often do so with a list of classical moral virtues such a courage, temperance, and justice. But there is a broader and more classical meaning of "virtue" such that *any* excellence is a virtue; that is, anything one is good at or an expert in is a virtue. Perhaps one is a fast runner, clever at solving puzzles, or is an excellent fly caster. These are virtues in this broader sense. Thus, there are intellectual virtues like mathematical reasoning, physical virtues such as running, and moral virtues, i.e., excellences in the area of ethics.

There are many definitions of "virtue," together with wide and deep debates concerning meanings and justifications.[2] A suitable definition of "virtue" will help in what follows. Linda Zagzebski defines a virtue in this way:

> *A virtue, then, can be defined as a deep and enduring acquired excellence of a person, involving a characteristic motivation to produce a certain desired end and reliable success in bringing about that end.*[3] <bolding by Zagzebski>

This definition is valuable because it is general enough to include moral and intellectual excellences as well as excellences in other skills. Notice two things about this definition. First, virtues are "acquired excellences" and we must add acquired in the course of participating in certain activities. That is, the "certain desired end" is that of an activity where others share this end and can thus help educate for this end.[4] Second, the "motivation," as we'll see in this chapter, comes from choosing activities for their own sakes. The activities best suited for choice are those discussed in the last chapter. These are activities that habituate excellence in practical reason, under the guidance of mentors, in the face of uncertainty.

Choosing Leisure Activities for Excellence

Aristotle makes much of the ethical power of the activities we participate in as young people and as adults. He believes that similar states of character will arise out of doing similar activities. Participating in activities forms habits and, under the guidance of good teachers, these habits may become excellences. Which activities we choose will have much to do with the states of character we get. Aristotle says:

> *Thus, in one word, states arise out of like activities. This is why the activities we exhibit must be of a certain kind; it is because the states correspond to the differences between these. It makes no small difference, then, whether we form habits of one kind or another from our very youth; it makes a very great difference, or rather all the difference.*[5]

If states of character are at least partially formed by the activities we choose for our children to engage in, we need to look closely at them. Aristotle finds those activities done "for their own sakes" to be connected to the development of virtue; he calls these "leisure." None of these, of course, are *intrinsically* leisure activities; we may *choose* to do them for their own sakes more or less. Someone may tie flies as a hobby but also sell them occasionally. A hunting guide might make a living by guiding others but might also hunt for its own sake. Activities become leisure based on our motives. Now, sometimes we call free or spare time leisure time. This is time away from work, time off. In this sense leisure is a recovery from and preparation for more work. It is rest and relaxation. Aristotle argues that leisure must be other than mere time off if it is to serve in the formation of character. For him, leisure is activity and not rest. Such leisure activities are closely connected with the development of virtue. When activities are pursued in this leisure state their end is excellence, which is the final end of human activity. Happiness is found in excellence.

So, leisure is not work or occupation because these are activities of necessity not performed for their own sakes.[6] Nor is leisure a preparation for or recovery from work. Such time of recovery and relaxation is indeed necessary in order to continue to work, but because this time is in the service of the end of continuing to work, it is not leisure. Nor is leisure mere play or amusement because if these are pursued for relaxation they are subservient to work, or if they are pursued for their own sake they betray a childish conception of happiness as pleasure. Rather, those activities chosen as ends in themselves are chosen in the desire to achieve excellence. Even though someone might claim that they participate in, for instance, birding because of the pleasure it gives them, Aristotle would understand this to mean that they experience pleasure as a byproduct in the pursuit of excellence.

For Aristotle, the activities undertaken in a state of leisure are primarily educational. Judith Swanson claims, with good reason, that "Aristotle means by 'leisure' the liberal arts or 'culture.'"[7] Aristotle's best-known examples of self-chosen liberating arts are music and philosophy. However, there is some evidence that he may include various sciences as well.[8] For the moment, the content of this leisure education is less important than the fact that classical leisure is closely connected with certain types of self-chosen educational activities.

Aristotle's most fully developed example of leisure is the participation in the production of music. Music, Aristotle argues, has "some influence over the character and the soul."[9] The process of learning music, dance, poetry, or theater is a many-stepped and perhaps lifelong process. Knowledge of theoretical principles will be necessary, and these will be brought to bear on the feelings occasioned by and infused into the music. These steps and stages start in youth and continue through adulthood. As Carnes Lord says:

> Aristotle's proof that the 'more honorable nature' of music is its power to educate or to affect the character and soul is at the same time a proof that the 'more honorable' activity of [leisure] . . . is a fundamentally 'ethical' or 'educative' activity.[10]

Why are those activities most capable of generating excellences leisure activities? It is because excellence is the sole reason one has for participating in them. Of course, some of us when we were young were *compelled* by our parents to participate in certain activities such as music lessons. We certainly didn't choose it for its own sake. Yet for some this forced march actually does become a leisure activity in the sense Aristotle discusses. That is, some students continue to pursue this difficult activity because of the pleasure and satisfaction it brings them. In these cases, one can imagine the student diligently practicing for the sake of the excellence achievable. The same student will seek out honest criticisms and fair competitions to evaluate progress. This is the self-chosen, slow, building of character. The equally slow building of excellence also requires relations with teachers and other musicians. At a later stage, as we shall see, the citizen-musician may realize that the activity chosen for its own sake requires certain social and political conditions, if it is to remain viable.

This, of course, is an idealized picture of a leisure activity, but the point I am trying to establish is that certain leisure activities do generate excellence. Certainly not all participants progress equally and for some, excellence remains elusive. But when we do something for its own sake the joy of this engagement is frequently characterized as "heightened" or total involvement; it is a kind of continuous happiness that Aristotle endorses. The special kind of pleasure associated with these activities continues so long as one is so engaged.

John Rawls in *A Theory of Justice* discusses what he calls the "Aristotelian Principle." It states that:

> *The intuitive idea here is that human beings take more pleasure in doing something as they become more proficient at it, and of two activities they do equally well, they prefer the one calling on a larger repertoire of more intricate and subtle discriminations.*[11]

This principle explains the motivation we have to continue in the pursuit of mastery and excellence. Leisure activities are directed at excellence, but they are also accompanied with the pleasure of doing things well.

The Virtues of Leisure

Certain leisure activities are richly endowed with the potential for the development of character.[12] Excellences or virtues are of several kinds. Besides the skills one might develop, there are moral virtues such as courage, intellectual virtues like mathematical and scientific reasoning, and civic virtues, which are required by one's relationships with members of the community in which one lives. When these virtues are smoothly articulated, a state of excellence is attained. This is the mark of character.

A finely developed practical reason under the guidance of mentors motivated by the pursuit of excellence is perfectly positioned to habituate yet other virtues. Judging by what Aristotle and others have said, moral virtues are those acquired by forming habits of the right sort. Certain activities are laden with opportunities for such habituation. Nearly every activity children engage in is thought to have some moral implications, be it at play, school, or home. It is also true that some activities are better than others at encouraging young people to practice making ethical choices. Sports have traditionally been included in this category, but not always.[13] On the other hand, some activities are pretty much devoid of such opportunities. As an extreme example, some players of video games find nothing wrong with using "cheats" to succeed at the game. There is apparently no reason not to use them. This is an ethically depleted activity; there's little opportunity to try out one's character. On the other hand, some activities offer a rich environment for moral character development. These activities by their nature present students of the activity with opportunities to exercise their ethical judgment. This is especially true of field sports among all the kinds and varieties of outdoor leisure activities. Field sports, after all, concern the ultimate ethical challenges of life and death. As we'll see in Chapters Six and Seven, these matters confront the participant with experiences so powerful they enable the formation of ethical virtues.

A second extension of one's character concerns those states of mind Aristotle calls intellectual virtues. These intellectual excellences are learned not by habituation but by speech or teaching. Some activities are brimming with opportunities in this area as well. Much self-motivated study is derived from some interest one has in, for instance, geology or music, bird identification or dog training. One interest often leads to another. Attending classes and demonstrations is sometimes part of the development of these intellectual virtues. This knowledge is scientific and theoretical.[14] Again field sports invite this extension in an intimate and dramatic way: the connections between one's quarry and the environmental conditions necessary for its flourishing become of central importance to hunters and anglers.

Finally, certain leisure activities require the "right kind of companionship."[15] There is the need for confirmation of progress and success by others who play the role of teachers, judges, and observers. The relationships developed with others in the joint participation in an art require that civic virtues become a part of one's character, because without these the community providing needed support for the activity would be unable to continue. The community of practitioners is itself surrounded by wider and more diffuse spheres of concern: social and political groups become important insofar as they have bearing on the continuation of the art. As Marcia Homiak says:

> *The key to the relationship between activity and virtue lies in understanding the sociopolitical conditions that serve to foster continuous activity. These conditions themselves require virtue.*[16]

One example may help us to understand this and see how it will connect with field sports. Suppose there is a certain defunct dam blocking the migration of fish on a stream that is important for spawning. The community of anglers who wish to see the dam removed must develop relations with lawyers, politicians, scientists, and other members of the community to see the process reach a successful conclusion in the removal of the dam. These ever-widening spheres require what Aristotle called civic virtues on the part of anglers.[17]

To make the connection between choosing activities for their own sakes and virtues, we should remember that the learning and application of skill is a use of *practical reasoning* as discussed in the last chapter. Practical reason is the precondition for the successful accomplishment of every skillful activity. That is, the process one goes through to become, for example, an expert fly angler synthesizes physical ability with background knowledge and a set of experiences such that one habitually makes the right cast at the right time. Yet casting a fly line, while called a skill, is really one thread in the whole fabric of fly fishing, i.e., one component of a skill which also includes the diagnosis and requisite background knowledge as well as the reliance on one's experience. So the actual skill of casting a fly line has its purpose solving a problem, which also brings to bear many other attendant skills.

Choosing activities for their own sakes—leisure activities— is explained by the desire to attain excellence. In trying to become excellent in some such area, one attains practical reasoning under the guidance of well-motivated mentors. Practical reasoning is "highly adaptive" because becoming good at practical reasoning in one area readily transfers to other areas.[18] Practical reason solves problems, whether they are in angling or ethics. The salient features are different but, under the instruction of well-motivated teachers, good habits are formed in both. The ability to reach correct practical decisions in, for example, solving a problem of navigation is the same ability one needs to solve a problem tracking an animal. The salient features are different, but the process is the same.[19] In the last chapter, we discussed reading the water and other natural sign reading that must be mastered. Surely these are some of the most highly adaptable skills one could mention. These are practice at what Aristotle (as referenced by Homiak) calls "gathering the meaning of things."

Aristotle calls the synthesis of these kinds of virtues into one's character a state of "perception." He says that determining that a person is morally blameworthy will "depend on particular facts, and the decision rests with perception."[20] That is, when we come to judge actions, our own or others, we will need access to particular facts relevant or salient to the case at hand. Experts "see" what is important to the case; they have the "eyes of wisdom." The opportunity to practice this capacity is found in the activities one engages in. This ability to focus on what is relevant for critical decisions needs to be practiced and refined. Certain activities offer this for the committed practitioner.[21]

One might still object that it is unclear how particular activities "give rise" to a *particular* set of virtues. The general categories of virtue just discussed leave this question open. As we will see, we decide on a particular list of virtues we wish to develop based upon the overall goals or ends we set. Then, we seek out activities that seem suitable to habituate those very virtues. Suppose we are interested as educators in the inculcation of several virtues. Then we look around for ways of inculcating these in our students. We see that several activities seem pretty good at habituating them. So we begin to teach students these activities. Now the philosopher will want to know what it is about these activities that leads to the actual development of those virtues. What is it about hunting and angling that lead to certain virtues? Well, one answer is just empirical. We say, "Look, Teddy Roosevelt was a great conservationist, and he was a hunter and an angler. So, those are the right activities to engage in if one wants to develop those virtues of conservation." But this argument is clearly self-serving and circular.

Something more than the empirical argument is needed. We need some map that takes us from activities to character development by reference to particular virtues generated.

We have established that it is at least *possible* for activities to generate virtues, even if the actual list of virtues remains to be found. Activities chosen for the sake of excellence offer us chances to test moral convictions, expand our knowledge and move toward wisdom, and sharpen our perception for the particulars needed to make critical judgments.

Conclusion

Understanding the sportsman thesis requires us to look first for characteristics of activities and second at the motivations for participation that then might be used to understand their presumed ability to generate character. We can't just leave the connection mysterious, as in that cartoon where a mathematician is putting formulas on the board, and, at one point writes "and then a miracle occurs" and continues with the proof. This is something like what has historically taken place with the sportsman thesis. We have field sports on the one hand, and "then a miracle occurs" and we have gentlemanly virtues blooming in abundance: courage, perseverance, sagacity, strength, activity, and caution, all of which are equally qualities of the "gentleman" and the sportsman.

To bridge this gap I have made the following argument. Activities with long histories of expertise, such as field sports, rely for their coherence on standards of skillfulness. Practical reason, the process of developing expertise, is achieved by practice under the guidance of well-intentioned mentors, in the face of stochastic difficulties. Practical reason, developed in the context of such activities, is highly adaptive and transferable from one context to another when salient features change. In activities chosen for their own sakes, i.e., leisure, the only relevant motive in this choice is the pursuit of excellence and the pleasure that attends its achievement. Virtues, in general, are habitual acquired excellences, motivated by a desire to bring about a certain end, measured by reliable success achieving that end. So, when we choose those select activities as a way of achieving excellence, we may reliably expect virtue development, including, given the adaptability of practical reason, moral and intellectual excellences.

The challenge we now face is to identify a particular list of these virtues, which together will determine the character of the contemporary sportsman.

Part Two
Environmental Virtues and Field Sports

The view I am proposing is one version of the sportsman thesis: that field sports when practiced properly will lead to the development of certain *environmental* virtues. These virtues, while seemingly lower in the pantheon than Platonic courage or Aristotelian sagacity, and even Roosevelt's manliness, have great importance in environmental ethics.

Environmental ethics is a field devoted to the applications of philosophical and moral theories to issues of environmental concern. The kinds of views one finds expressed in this field vary widely and there is as yet no consensus as to which approach is best suited to solve the environmental problems at hand. One emerging view is that virtue ethics will provide the guidance necessary to do so.[1] This is the approach I shall follow.

Virtue ethics in general and environmental virtue ethics in particular must successfully answer three questions to be adequate. These questions will motivate the discussion in Part Two.

First, what is the good aimed at? While virtues are thought of as goods in themselves, they are also a part of greater things, perhaps the good life or the good society. This, at least, is what Aristotle argues, and I think he is right. He says that the goal or good of human life is happiness, which he characterizes as human flourishing. And he also argues that in order for this to occur we must seek to develop virtue and also live in certain kinds of societies. An evaluation of the vast literature and controversy devoted to these topics will be left to others. Here, the first question becomes what good guides the choice for *environmental* virtues. In Chapter Four, I will track the way the goal aimed at by the sportsman thesis has been modified since the days of Teddy Roosevelt. This history will allow us to recognize a new goal: the biotic good. I will argue that the good of the *biotic* community—in particular its integrity, stability, and beauty, to use Leopold's terms—is what must guide our choice of virtues in this realm. Then, in Chapter Five, I will detail what this goal entails as a way of narrowing our search for the proper list of environmental virtues.

The second question, then, faced by environmental virtue ethics, is what specific list of virtues is required to meet the goal or bring about the good identified in response to the first question. This is also a matter of significant disagreement among philosophers.[2] In Chapter Six, I will argue that there are three virtues required for the good of biotic diversity: an ecological conscience, environmental awareness, and aesthetic competence. These three virtues are integral to Leopold's land ethic.

The third question faced by environmental virtue ethics is how the virtues chosen to bring about the good required are actually generated. That is, which activities will encourage people to develop the virtues of an ecological conscience, environmental awareness, and aesthetic competence? My answer is obvious at this point: we teach them field sports in the right way.[3]   I will begin to answer this question more thoroughly in Chapter Six, but the complete view will require that we attend to certain problems in Part Three.

The traditional sportsman thesis boldly asserts that certain virtues will arise from the practice of field sports. However, it leaves unexplained, among other things, the way this might actually happen. The sportsman thesis does posit a brief answer to the question of which good is served, namely, the good of being a gentleman. If we must give up the notion of becoming a gentleman, perhaps we can at least become environmentally virtuous. So, let's begin with the first question of virtue ethics, namely, what good is targeted that explains the list of virtues we'd like to generate? That is, what do we hope to achieve by encouraging people to develop virtues?

Conserving Animals

With Teddy Roosevelt and Gifford Pinchot at the peak of their influence at the beginning of the twentieth century, the sportsman was still very much a gentleman, presumably desiring all or most of the attendant virtues. But, because it was obvious that game animals were disappearing at an alarming rate, sportsmen soon realized that they had the additional task of "conservation."[1] The meaning of this much-debated term at this early point in time was simply to preserve game species for future hunters and anglers.[2] Leopold notes, in his 1933 essay "The Conservation Ethic," that the perceived goal of conservation was merely "to save species from extermination."[3] He continues: "the means to this end were a series of restrictive enactments" on hunting and angling.[4]

Sportsmen should voluntarily adhere to limits but those other non-sporting hunters will have to be compelled by law and social pressure. The sportsmen knew that for their activity to continue something had to be done to reestablish animal populations severely depleted by years of overhunting and habitat loss. The sportsmen were well placed to effect a change. They were often politically well connected and wealthy. They were members of exclusive hunting and angling clubs, and they were highly motivated because of the obvious declines in game numbers.

Conservation, therefore, meant for these sportsmen the need to save game species from extinction and, if possible, to increase their numbers. This goal began to be accomplished in several ways. First, not only did these sportsmen lobby for limits on the number of animals taken, and the seasons during which they may be taken, but they also, secondly, attempted to set themselves off from non-sporting hunters.[5] These other market and "pot hunters" were denigrated in the sporting press because of their lack of restraint, unsporting methods, and general lack of class.

The agenda for making this policy work was fairly obvious if difficult to achieve. It involved instituting a social and political movement against wasteful hunting and fishing. This was accomplished by getting laws passed enacting seasons and limits, banning the interstate sale of wildlife, and vilifying the hunters who violated these and other restrictions. This later vilification was carried out in the sporting press at the time.[6]

Conservation was thus spliced onto the sportsman thesis in response to unbridled exploitation of animals by hunters and fishermen. To counteract this exploitation, a virtue was added to the list of gentlemanly virtues: restraint. This was already implicit in some versions of the sportsman thesis. For instance, the minister John Mason Peck, in his hagiography of Daniel Boone, says hunting taught Boone self-possession and self-control.[7] Clearly self-control implies restraint, and it is this virtue that bears the weight of conservation at this point.

Leopold and the Sportsman Thesis

It is evident that Aldo Leopold is introduced to the sportsmanship thesis early in his life, by his father but also by his own reading of Roosevelt and Stuart Edward White.[8] But with Leopold we witness a radical change in the content and purpose of the thesis. In response to both intellectual tensions and practical difficulties, Leopold finds it necessary to alter the sportsman thesis in a way that keeps the educational core of virtue generation and yet changes the actual virtues generated. He does so by shifting the good to be served. Whereas the traditional sportsmanship thesis had as its good the development of young gentlemen, and Roosevelt added that goal of conservation, Leopold expands the goal yet again to the "good of the biotic community."

Leopold realizes that the problem of diminishing game can only be successfully solved by expanding the reach of the sportsman thesis in several ways. If the goal of game abundance is added to that of becoming a gentleman, as suggested by Roosevelt, field sports must be regulated by more than a mere impulse to conserve on the part of hunters and anglers only.[9] No matter how many limitations sportsmen place on *themselves*, game populations will need help from federal and state governments and, even more importantly, private landowners. Seasons must be enforced and limits monitored. Animal populations must be tracked and restocked where necessary. In addition, the practices of private landowners, such as farming, logging, and ranching, have crucial repercussions for animal populations. Leopold sees that the self-regulation of the sportsman-conservationist must be supplemented and backed with the state-sanctioned power of enforcement and, of equal importance, some way to convince private landowners of the value of wildlife.[10] Leopold realizes that state regulation by itself is never sufficient to resolve environmental problems involving game animals, and in some ways it may actually harm these populations. The conscience of farmers, loggers, and private landowners in general must be engaged if the problem of disappearing game is to be resolved. Thus the goal of the sportsman thesis must be expanded to include non-sportsmen.

The health of game populations depends upon more than even the most fervent commitments of sportsmen. There is the clear need for governmental involvement in maintaining game populations. But even professionals can't do it all. So, private landowners must also be brought to recognize the importance of conservation. Leopold, while not opposed to governmental involvement in conservation, sees it as in principle insufficient. He worries that when conservation is solely the task of government, then a downward cycle is inevitable:

> *The fallacy inherent in this policy has already been pointed out: There is nothing to prevent all our vulnerable land from eventually running through the same sequence of private deterioration followed by public repairs.*[11]

If private landowners share no sense of obligation to the land, the cycle of destruction will continue.

Besides the need to expand the appeal for conservation beyond sportsmen, a second insight motivates Leopold. His research in ecology led him to the conclusion that environmental policies and practices must take account of the biotic community as a whole and not one species or another. The conservation of Roosevelt was too narrowly focused on game animals with little awareness of the way their flourishing depends upon the health of the biotic community in which they reside. Thus the goal sought by the sportsman thesis is itself expanded from a concern for game animals to a concern for the biotic community in which they reside.[12]

Leopold realizes the potency of the sportsman thesis and redirects it toward the goal of biotic conservation. The new goal of the sportsman thesis invites not only hunters and anglers, but private landowners and wildlife professionals as well. The good aimed at and the virtues generated must be understood and made available to a much wider audience. Leopold calls this a "new ideology," which enlists hunters and anglers as agents of environmental preservation. As he notes, "this new idea is so far regarded as merely a new and promising means to better hunting and fishing but its potential uses are much larger."[13] Much larger indeed!

Conclusion

Whereas the sportsman thesis had once merely encompassed the goal of being a gentleman, it then evolved to address the need to conserve game animal populations. But Leopold believes this addition is simply insufficient to its task. The mere imposition of restrictions in the form of game laws and limits does not address several forces contributing to the decline in game populations, let alone other environmental problems. Private landowners like farmers, ranchers, and loggers must be somehow persuaded to contribute to the cause. Also, governmental agencies willing myopically to restock and replant must be influenced. Those industries that rely on wild resources must also be offered ethical guidance. Politically, Leopold sees hunters and anglers as the first line of defense in this movement. They already have an ethical basis in the sportsman thesis and they are motivated by self-interest to preserve game animals. However, even for Leopold's sportsmen, there is little sense of the broader requirements of the health of the community in which these populations will either thrive or perish. For Leopold there are no substitutes for the land ethic.

Leopold's need to alter the sportsman thesis is understandable, but is it reasonable? Is environmental virtue ethics capable of incorporating the change? We shall need to explore the way his land ethic alters the goal of the sportsman thesis in the direction of the biotic good.

Chapter Five: The Biotic Good

The question we must now confront is how field sports might be directed toward a new good, one that will require significant sacrifices. What is the good of the biotic community and how might field sports be directed to bring about this good? In terms of virtues, which list is most appropriate for the good of the biotic community and how might it be enabled by field sports? In order to answer these questions, we will first explore the central principle of the land ethic. Secondly, we will define the biotic community. And finally, this community will provide the context needed to explain the new virtues to be engendered by field sports.

The Principle of the Land Ethic

Much of Leopold's contribution to the evolution of the sportsman thesis is due to his articulation of a new good that requires a new list of virtues associated with hunting. This new good is expressed in his famous principle of the land ethic: "A thing is right when it tends to preserve the integrity, stability, and beauty of the biotic community. It is wrong when it tends otherwise."[1] I will explain two parts of this principle in this section. First, by addressing the question of what is meant by a "thing" that is right? This will help us understand the scope of the principle. Second, the list of properties: integrity, stability, and beauty will be examined. These properties will be connected with the environmental virtues developed by field sports. There are many other controversies surrounding the interpretation of the principle that I will not explore because they lead us into complex issues in ethical theory, such as the inherent value of nature.[2]

Let's be clear about what "things" are right or wrong. It is my belief that what Leopold means by "things" are those arts or practices that either acquire goods from or produce goods by way of biotic communities. So hunting, fishing, farming, logging, mining, etc. are all included. So are policies advocated by both governmental and non-governmental agencies, such as the now abandoned plan to extirpate wolves or the continuing policy of stocking streams with non-native fish. Individual actions are rarely included; it's the big picture that is evaluated by this principle. In an earlier version of this principle, Leopold actually uses the phrase "practices of conservation" in place of "things."[3] So while the principle has quite wide application, it is certainly not universal. Many activities simply don't fall under its purview, but surely field sports do.

Secondly, we need to come to understand integrity, stability, and beauty as properties that need to be preserved. On the one hand, it is reasonable to collect them all together under the label of "diversity." Each of the three properties is linked by Leopold to diversity. For instance, he says: "Diversity . . . means a food chain aimed to harmonize the wild and the tame in the joint interest of stability, productivity, and beauty."[4] The good of the biotic community is determined by its diversity. Hunters, Leopold says, cannot "love game and hate predators." Predators are part of the necessary diversity of the biotic community. Diversity remains the good of the biotic community even though we as yet do not understand very well how such diversity works. Indeed, we might conclude that it is our very ignorance of the inner workings of the biotic community that demands we respect its diversity.

On the other hand, if Leopold simply meant "diversity" as the property to be preserved, why didn't he just say so instead of complicating matters with three additional concepts? I therefore think there is something important in his choice of "integrity, stability, and beauty."

Integrity is a term that has both ethical and material meanings. A bridge might fail to have integrity and so might a politician. What is meant is that the bridge is unable to withstand the stresses it will likely be subject to and the politician's character will be unlikely to withstand the temptations and compromises he or she will face. Integrity is in both cases a matter of strength in the face of adversity. Biotic communities undergo continuous stress, both from human and non-human sources. The eruption of a volcano, a forest fire, and a flood, are all tests of the integrity of a biotic community. So too do activities such as farming, logging, building suburbs, or contributing to acid rain. Surely hunting and angling also test the integrity of a biotic community, or its ability to continue to be "productive"—another word used as a substitute for integrity by Leopold. To what degree will a biotic community withstand these stresses? Will it remain healthy during and after use? In this context, to ask if an activity is "sustainable" is just another way of asking about the integrity of a given biotic community.[5]

Leopold sometimes links the concept of integrity with that of *stability*, as in the following:

> *Yet these creatures [of no economic value] are members of the biotic community, and if (as I believe) its stability depends on its integrity, they are entitled to continuance.*[6]

Here Leopold is attempting to establish a reason for valuing species with no *economic* value, such as song birds or insects, and he appeals to both stability and integrity in his argument. From the observation that plant and animal species form essential links in many food chains, he infers that the stability of the whole community is dependant on the complexity and length of those chains. Stability is enhanced by multiple and complex links in these chains; the chains that have been forged by evolution over eons. Can there be anything more stable than this? As we shorten these chains, or substitute others, we tend to unbalance the biotic community. Using stability as a measure asks us to consider the ways in which our activities alter relationships formed by evolution. Stability does not mean stasis, but it does use the test of evolutionary survival over long periods of time.

The inclusion of *beauty* as a property of the biotic community is somewhat surprising given the standard view that it is "in the eye of the beholder." There is a large body of literature concerning "nature aesthetics," most of which I will place in the background.[7] What we need to consider, relative to field sports, is that certain policies and practices tend to enhance sportsmen's aesthetic competence for judgments about the beauty of the biotic community, while others do not.[8] For instance, those policies and practices of conservation that encourage the appreciation of native species over non-native contribute to this competence. Ponds in the Adirondack Mountains of New York sometimes need to be reclaimed from their non-native fish species in order to reestablish native brook trout populations. This is a contribution to the beauty of the biotic community even though, for everyone but the aesthetically competent angler, things will look pretty much the same. Beauty is not in the eye of the beholder but in the diversity of the biome.[9]

Indeed, Leopold frequently contrasts the aesthetic value of the biotic community with its economic value in order to establish the existence of non-monetary obligations. This contrast between economic value and other kinds of value is basic for understanding the land ethic and the good of the biotic community. Leopold is searching high and low for any means to modify the power of the economic forces at work on the land. He sees all decisions about diversity and health of the biotic community wrongly subsumed by the power of economic value. His appeal to land ethics and land aesthetics is his effort to turn the economic tide. He realizes that economics will always have an important say in these decisions, but, as he says just before articulating the above principle, "Examine each question in terms of what is ethically and esthetically right, as well as what is economically expedient."[10] What it means to be aesthetically right will be a concern when we come to examine the new list of virtues and the way field sports might inculcate them. For now, we should keep in mind that all three of these properties are ways of looking at diversity and the effects various practices and policies have on it.

The Biotic Community

What exactly is the biotic community that we are asked to preserve in the principle of the land ethic? This is a crucial question because it is the *good* of this community that will explain the list of environmental virtues that will alter the sportsman thesis. Leopold realizes that the idea is amorphous at best and needs some sort of image to represent it. He says:

> An ethic to supplement and guide the economic relation to land presupposes the existence of some mental image of land as a biotic mechanism. We can be ethical only in relation to something we can see, feel, understand, love, or otherwise have faith in.[11]

The land pyramid illustrates one solution to this problem as well as provides a rich analogy. It has at its lowest level soils and water upon which are layered those plant and animal species that depend directly upon them. As we move up the pyramid, the food chains become clearer: predator-prey relations, relations of cooperation, relations of domestication, etc. Leopold places humans in the land pyramid in an "intermediate layer with the bears, raccoons, and squirrels which eat both meat and vegetables."[12] The image of a three-sided pyramid is helpful here. The three sides, or facets, can be thought of as representing the three aspects or properties mentioned above: integrity, stability, and beauty. The bottom of the pyramid, which unifies the three sides can be thought of as diversity. Looking into the pyramid through any of these facets reveals the same sets of ecological relations but from different perspectives.

The importance of this image with regard to environmental virtue will be discussed in the next chapter. However, there are three critical questions to be answered in what follows: How are we to judge what really constitutes the "good" of the biotic community? What happens when there is a conflict between the perceived good of the biotic community and the good of the human community? And is there really a biotic *community* in the first place?[13]

To answer the first question, the good of the biotic community is its diversity. We can know this even though we may not know the exact ways in which this diversity contributes to the good of the biotic community. Hunters and anglers must be constantly aware of the effects their practices have on diversity, as well as the image of diversity they seek to establish. The commitment to conservation, the harmonious relation of man and land as Leopold says, requires much more than the narrow care for "the deer herd" or the population of Canada geese. We, together with these species of animals are part of a complex web, which must be sustained as well. The good of the biotic community must determine the conservation efforts of field sports, if they are to maintain their moral significance. Diversity is not harmed by the death of individual game animals, but the practices of hunting and angling have the potential to seriously undermine diversity if not regulated by the land ethic.

The second question concerns the inevitable conflicts that occur between the needs of the human community and those of the biotic community. Which takes precedence? As I've pointed out above, the land ethic is designed to deal with environmental or conservation practices. Other, broader, ethical views, such as traditional virtue ethics, are compatible with the land ethic and those must be charged with general concerns about human ethical conflicts. Resolution of the specific conflicts between humans and other members of the biotic community is a huge topic. It will be addressed in future chapters in a more specific form: how do we resolve conflicts between sportsmen concerning the best policies for the biotic community. However, what is important at this point is the third question, which is best answered by saying that some people do see a biotic community, and some, unfortunately, do not.[14] Sportsmen and others, whose activities take them afield, will and must have a very strong perception of the biotic community.

Now, how do we move from a goal that requires the preservation of the integrity, stability, and beauty of the biotic community to a list of virtues that might replace those first articulated in the sportsman thesis? This is the project of the next chapter.

Conclusion

The biotic good is the integrity, stability, and beauty of the community. Conservation practices must aim at this goal. These practices are not just field sports, but also include farming, logging, and ranching; in addition those professional practices of conservation found in state and federal agencies must also direct their efforts to this goal. The three perspectives provided by integrity, stability, and beauty are unified in the concept of diversity, and they evoke values to mitigate the standard economic model.

Chapter Six: Environmental Virtues

I have argued that field sports are the kinds of activities capable of generating virtue. There are two broad conditions necessary for attaining this status. First, such activities must be teachers of practical reasoning, the precondition for virtue formation. Certainly, the problem solving of field sports fits this model. In Chapter Two, we examined this role of practical reason in developing expertise: making good diagnostic decisions in the face of uncertainties and being able to act on them at the right time in the right way. Whether the skill is navigation, medicine, hunting, or angling, the same educational goals of expertise are present. The education of practical reason trains one's diagnostic ability based on sufficient background knowledge, the experience and skill to habitually perform the right actions, and finally as a consequence of these, the expert's summative ability to just "see" what needs to be done. The connection between practical reason and the possibility of virtue generation lies in its ultimate adaptability to other circumstances and the educational need for mentorship in the face of unpredictable circumstances.

Second, virtue-generating activities are chosen for their own sakes, which means, so I've argued, for the sake of excellence. Participants are motivated by their desire for the pleasures and satisfactions that accompany their pursuit of excellences or virtues. In Chapter Three, I noted that hunting and fishing are lifelong, self-chosen activities for some of us. The character building that we begin in childhood is expected to continue throughout our lives. Expertise is a constant goal, and the difficulties in achieving it are apparent. The pursuit of excellence encourages us to understand the various stages necessary for its achievement. Those character-enriching activities are leisure activities where, besides the practical problems, e.g., which fly to use, one also faces ethical challenges and intellectual puzzles. One's success in solving these problems and puzzles depends on practice under the supervision of a community of like-minded people. Excellences of moral and intellectual character are developed right alongside of those other excellences of skill and expertise, given the right guidance.

So, field sports are *capable* of generating excellences, as claimed by the sportsman thesis, if chosen for the right reasons and taught in the right way. But the good served by field sports is not *just* that of excellence of the participant. There must be an environmental goal as well: the biotic good. Now, any specific list of desirable virtues is ultimately arrived at by considerations of the desired goals and ends of activities. As I argued in the previous two chapters, this goal has correctly been shifted for field sports from the pursuit of a gentlemanly status, then to an old-style, game-animal-centered conservation, and finally to the preservation of the biotic good. Once this shift is accepted, we are in a position to identify a list of excellences field sports should inculcate in their practitioners to serve this end. Happily, to some extent we will find that these environmental virtues are already present in field sports, but my point will be that field sports must, if they are to maintain an environmentally secure ethical base, be redirected as far as possible to bring these virtues about.

This chapter will identify these virtues and point out actual instances of them in the literature of field sports. The remaining issues of making these virtues more precise and modifying field sports to inculcate these virtues will be addressed in Parts Three and Four.

Three Components of the Land Ethic

The good of the biotic community, as discussed in the last chapter, will guide us in identifying several environmental virtues necessary for its preservation. If the educational goal of field sports is excellence and the ecological goal is the biotic good, as Leopold believes, then we need to determine which habits or excellences we wish young people and adults to develop which will serve these goals. In order to make this a bit more concrete, consider once again the image of the land pyramid. As I explained in Chapter Five, the components of the land ethic can be represented as three sides or facets of the land pyramid. Let us use Leopold's terms for these three facets: integrity, stability, and beauty. They are three lenses for focusing on the diversity of the complex whole or the biotic good. I believe these windows determine which list of virtues will serve the biotic good. Practices and activities that influence and depend upon the biotic community in significant ways should be refined to develop in their participants virtues related to these facets.

Ideally, when young anglers and hunters face tests of their nascent ethical sense, their lack of skills, knowledge, and experience will be compensated for by the guidance of others. There are the temptations of technological shortcuts to skill—hoggishness, carelessness, and other immoderate behaviors. Young people are in the process of developing an *ecological conscience* regarding natural things, a process that continues through life. Perhaps at a later stage, some become curious about the natural processes by which animals flourish or diminish; they seek knowledge of animal and plant life cycles and ecological requirements. They wonder how things got to be the way they are by evolution and human intervention. They take an interest in the biotic community of which they are members. What is the relation between healthy brook trout populations and stream temperatures and water clarity? Which kinds of landscapes are best for grouse? This more or less scientific or *environmental awareness* is often driven both by desire for successful hunting and angling as well as sheer curiosity.

Finally, in addition to an ethically tested conscience and a budding curiosity about the natural world, some develop a more or less explicit aesthetic response to the natural world, one that goes beyond the mere "pretty" as Leopold says. What are the right emotional responses? What is of value in the experiences we have? This is the development of what I will call the virtue of *aesthetic competence*.[1]

When questions of this sort are answered we might eventually develop a unified perception of the biotic community. Our knowledge is synthesized with our concern for natural things, awareness with emotional response, and curiosity with reverence. This perception of natural things is evaluative and critical of the experiences we have. A stable environmental character is the same as a correctly focused perception of the biotic community. Thus the virtues I will discuss individually are in practice unified and mutually supporting.

Field sports, properly taught and ecologically aligned, provide an opportunity for growth: emotionally, intellectually, and ethically. This is a constant in the sportsman thesis. What is new is that the excellences or virtues are sought within the context of the good of the biotic community. This is why they are called environmental virtues. Only seen in this way will field sports retain their relevance and remain in the good graces of those who are, so far, reserving judgment.

Ecological Conscience

The term "ecological conscience" is introduced by Leopold as a way of counter-balancing an extreme economic and self-interested approach to environmental decision making. He realizes that economic factors will always be important but thinks we have gone too far in that direction. He says that conservation is a kind of harmony between humans and the land. One way this harmony is thrown off balance is when economic or other kinds of self-interest become the dominant force in environmental decision making. As a habit, an ecological conscience balances individual self-interest and more broadly human-centered concerns against the integrity of the biotic pyramid. Immoderate self-interest is a too keen need for external rewards of many kinds, one of which is economic gain. As we shall see, other external factors that throw this balance off are fame or honors granted by others, various trophies, and need for proofs of accomplishment. These external rewards, like economic gain, skew the balance required for an ecological conscience. Striking this balance is clearly desirable and necessary for the preservation of the integrity of the biotic good. The problem is how this might be accomplished and whether field sports are capable of effecting the change.

This task, so ethically central, might be thought to be too great for field sports to accomplish. Leopold knows that an ecological conscience might be generated in different outdoor activities, and is thus quite adaptable to other "practices of conservation" as well. He mentions, for instance, farmers who decide to attempt to return part of their farmland to native plant species. This kind of restoration project, he believes, both reflects and deepens a new conscience. He contrasts this with that kind of farming dominated by mere economic self-interest, and thus one that needs to be balanced by an ecological conscience. However, the decision to restore native plants is not only motivated by pangs of conscience, but also depends crucially on what one knows and how one feels about the look of one's farm.[2] As adults, these farmers have achieved that kind of integration that we will come to call perception. Or maybe they are on their way to this. What is important is that certain activities, for instance farming, are well suited to develop virtue.[3]

So, field sports are not the *only* paths to the ecological conscience. Other areas in need of an ecological conscience are the professions of forestry and wildlife management, according to Leopold. Each of these areas is faced with what he calls the "AB cleavage," which divides those who regard the land as a commodity producer and those who regard it as a biota. The latter group, Leopold thinks, "feels the stirrings of an ecological conscience."[4]

When it comes to field sports, Leopold is also critical of unrestrained self-interest.

> *It cannot be right, in the ecological sense, for the deer hunter to maintain his sport by browsing out the forest, or for the bird hunter to maintain his by decimating the hawks and owls, or for the fisherman to maintain his by decimating the herons, kingfishers, terns, and otters. Such tactics seek to achieve one kind of conservation by destroying another, and thus they subvert the integrity and stability of the community.*[5]

Happily, some of these practices have disappeared since Leopold wrote, but not all. Some hunters and anglers lack the balance of an ecological conscience. They are driven by self-interest and thus are willing to "maintain their sport" in ecologically harmful ways—for example, strenuously opposing predator re-introduction plans because they would tend to reduce the numbers of game animals to some extent. This attitude is to be expected. But field sports have the capacity to mitigate this vice. If youthful skills are practiced under the supervision of perceptive mentors—teachers of practical reason—and if the participant is motivated by a search for excellence, and, finally, when the setting is ethically laden as it is in field sports, then, such participants will develop an ecological conscience.

In the above quote, when Leopold writes of one kind of conservation destroying another, he means to say that the balance necessary for the ecological conscience is destroyed by such tactics. There is, for example, a tendency among some hunters and anglers to personally decide for everybody the make-up of the biotic community. The (illegal) practice of moving a non-native species of fish into a body of water inhabited by another native kind is an extreme form of self-interest. In the American

West, this sometimes means the private stocking of brook trout in the same waters with cutthroat trout. In the East, sometimes brown trout are stocked where they don't belong. This is a matter of conscience for hunters and anglers and should be as well for professionals in the fish and wildlife departments. These professionals are sometimes torn between the perceived need to provide "recreational opportunities" to everyone and the knowledge that such approaches are ecologically suspect.

An education in field sports often introduces young people to the "doctrine of fair chase." Fair chase is sometimes defined as a method of pursuit that allows animals the chance to escape with sufficient frequency.[6] While we will examine this doctrine critically later, what is important, educationally, is that an ecological conscience is further habituated when this doctrine is followed. This "chance for animals" is increased by lessening our dependence on the use of finders and gadgets and increasing one's own skills of observation and movement. Hunting over bait and shooting sitting birds have long been decried as violations of the "code of the sportsman." These are violations because they are skill shortcuts. Finding game and shooting on the wing are skills that take great commitment of time, and one's expertise in these is a sign of this commitment. Setting these as goals for young sportsmen and following their progress is training in acquiring an ecological conscience.

Another example of a vice that displays a lack of skill is "snagging" fish, or the intentional foul-hooking of fish. This once-common practice is now legally banned in places. However, banned or not, it is still quite common to see it practiced on spawning salmon. One casts a weighted hook over the visible fish and gives the rod a good jerk when the hook is in the vicinity of the fish. The hook may become embedded in the fin or flesh of the salmon. This practice calls for little skill when compared to actually trying to get the salmon to eat the fly or bait. Clearly there is an educational choice to be made here.

For hunters and anglers both young and old, restraint is challenged by the burgeoning market for outdoor leisure gadgets. Leopold admonishes hunters and anglers for their reliance on store-bought and market-driven aids. He simply could not have imagined how bad things would become. The balance required by an ecological conscience is inhibited by over reliance on gadgets. Yet, Leopold worries that such unrestrained behavior will destroy the personal and public value of hunting and angling. To the degree that gadgets make hunting or angling too easy, they throw off the delicate balance sought by an ecological conscience.[7]

An ecological conscience develops in response to ethical challenges presented by participation in field sports. The quality of this conscience will depend both on the circumstances confronted and the guidance available. Field sports present myriad opportunities for ethical growth, more so than many other outdoor activities. If pursued and taught by hunters and anglers keenly aware of these opportunities, this virtue will grow.

What then is an ecological conscience? It is the counterbalance to the power of economic and other self-interested rewards in matters of conservation. It is stimulated by overcoming the temptations to cheat and seek approval. An ecological conscience requires constant practice, as does hitting any target. As in any application of practical reasoning, only by erring on one side and then the other does the ecological conscience achieve stability. Some standard moral virtues, such as restraint and respect, are used by others to make more familiar this ideal of an ecological conscience.[8] This is appropriate, because restraint is indeed necessary to resist the pull of the extremes. But an ecological conscience, while crucial to the character of the sportsman, is not by itself sufficient. Intellectual virtues are also a necessary part of one's character, and for Leopold, prime among them is knowledge or awareness of ecological and evolutionary relations.

Environmental Awareness

The stability of the biotic community encompasses the links forged by evolution, the critical role of humans, and the way culture and wilderness interact. Again, the image of the land pyramid will help us to see that this community is a "whole," in that its health and diversity depend on the relations between the various levels of the pyramid. Environmental awareness is a holistic understanding of the biotic community, driven by curiosity about the natural world and the practical necessities of successfully acquiring game animals. Leopold makes the point this way:

> I think we have here the root of the problem. What conservation education must build is an ethical underpinning for land economics and a universal curiosity to understand the land mechanism. Conservation may then follow.[9]

An ethical underpinning is provided by ecological conscience and curiosity is supported by environmental awareness. We are a part of this land mechanism and need to become fully aware of this fact, not as a scientific abstraction on the one hand nor as a self-regulating "mother nature" figure on the other. Indeed, the virtue of environmental awareness is a counterbalance for either too little reliance on science or too much.[10] The method of hitting this mean explains both the difficulty and the rewards of environmental awareness.

I previously appealed to the usefulness of "reading the water" in trout fishing or, more generally, "reading natural signs" as examples of a kind of holistic awareness of nature. Sometimes in field sports one just starts to "see" where animals might be by observing the signs. The verb "reading" is a bit too academic in these cases. But it is an impressive skill. The narrator of *Dersu the Trapper*, a fictional account of a paragon of environmental awareness, says: "For this astonishing man there were no secrets." The depth and complexity of such knowledge becomes immediately apparent if such an expert is asked to explain the belief that "there is a fish right there." The proper response to this is, "well, do you have a couple of days?" Or, as Dersu tersely exclaims: "How you not know? Look self!"[11] For those who participate in field sports, this comment will be familiar. As we become more adept at the activity, we just seem better able to see things, aware of what's relevant to our quest. The expansion of this knowledge to ever greater spheres of the biotic community starts and is practiced in field sports. For instance, an interest in catching fish on worms leads to raising fishing worms. An interest in catching fish on flies leads to raising chickens for their feathers. An interest in hunting woodcock leads to woodcock study and habitat restoration. This kind of knowledge does not require college degrees, as professor Leopold pointed out. Nor does it even need much acquaintance with books. It does require hours and hours of close observation, usually under the guidance of someone who already knows what's what. This expertise in finding fish or game can be promoted by small, unaware steps to a fully realized environmental awareness.

This kind of awareness, hard won from experience and mentoring, is far superior to that passive and glossy knowledge many people gain from watching wildlife on nature shows. This seems to be an increasingly appealing choice for television and movie watchers. Maybe it's the high definition. In these dramas, accompanied by appropriate sound tracks produced in sound studios, one hears fake chomps, scratches, and yelps while encountering the strange beauty of wildlife safely behind the television's window. Just as meat comes safely packaged in clear plastic, so we see but can't touch, on-screen wildlife comes packaged and predigested for us.

Environmental knowledge at this extreme is a kind of knowledge based on "just-so" stories, or what one recent book calls the method of "emotional imagination and narrative."[12] This is indeed an approach to wildlife that has much appeal to children and unconnected, de-natured adults. But "unconnected" is the operative word here. True environmental awareness seeks to make us appreciate the very real connections we have to the biotic community, whether we wish to acknowledge them or not.

At the other extreme is an approach to environmental awareness that is roundly criticized by Leopold, but is still a strong attraction. It is the thoroughly scientific approach to knowledge that Leopold lambastes as mere "cat carving." He has in mind the way in which natural history has been supplanted by laboratory science so our children learn about the natural world by memorizing the bumps on the bones of cats. Students end up with knowledge of small pieces of nature but with no understanding of the whole. This understanding of the land-community cannot be allotted to the guardianship of scientists alone: "Wildlife research started as a professional priest craft. . . . In the biological field, the sport-value of amateur research is just beginning to be realized."[13]

Leopold recognizes the role of leisure in providing pleasure and happiness but knows that the value of these activities must be found in their ability to generate character. This value is distorted by "modern machinery," which provides shortcuts to mastery and excellence. To use "modern mentality," by contrast, is to attempt to achieve environmental awareness in the pursuit of field sports. The relationship between human well-being and our appreciation of the natural world is apparent to amateur naturalists and students who are lucky enough, as Leopold says, to be educated in the relations plants, animals, soils, and water have to each other. Leopold simply calls this science ecology. At one point he asks, "What is our educational system doing to encourage personal amateur scholarship in the natural-history field?"[14] The skepticism expressed here regarding typical science curricula contrasts with Leopold's hope for environmental awareness as something we can all have and enjoy. His examples of an industrial chemist's pastime pursuit of the demise of passenger pigeons and an Ohio housewife's passion for understanding song sparrows clearly imply that such amateur scholarship is a potent vehicle for the development of environmental awareness.[15]

Now that the virtue of environmental awareness is clearer, we see how it is that field sports might generate it. Field sports invite and reward nature study. If one fishes for trout, there is every reason to study insects, stream-flow characteristics, and water quality. These are then integratd into that ability to read natural signs. This growth in environmental awareness is obvious to the reflective angler. It is also obvious in the writings of anglers. The incremental spread of one's interests from merely catching the fish to knowing everything about the fish's biotic place is illustrated in the writings of master anglers past and present.[16] If one hunts, then, natural connections between plants, trees, and minerals will occupy important places in one's mental archives. Equally important, these are not separate but unified in their relation to one's quarry. There is no better way to learn about the food chains one is part of, than by participating in field sports.[17]

Aesthetic Competence

Leopold uses the term "perception" in at least two ways, one broad and one narrow. The broad meaning is synonymous with that ideal of having a fully formed environmentally conscious character, with all the attendant virtues carefully honed and smoothly articulated. Leopold illustrates this broader kind of perception when he writes: "The swoop of a hawk . . . is perceived by one as the drama of evolution. To another it is only a threat to a full frying-pan." He continues: "To promote perception is the only truly creative part of recreational engineering."[18] The general problem is how one might move from seeing the hawk as a threat to game birds (or chickens) to the broader ecological vision of the hawk and the game bird as actors in the drama of evolution. This is the task of forming, i.e., recreationally engineering, the environmental characters of sportsmen. In this sense, perception is another term for the unified character including an ecological conscience and environmental awareness.

On the other hand, Leopold also uses a narrower conception of perception as an "aesthetic competence" that needs to be refined in young sportsmen and others.[19] Leopold compares this kind of perception to that of other refinements of emotional response generatd by the arts: "The taste for country displays the same diversity in *aesthetic competence* among individuals as the taste for opera, or oils."[20] It is surely true that there is a great diversity here of likes and dislikes of taste regarding fine arts. The problem is that watching an opera and looking at oil paintings are typically not activities involving participation and performance, even though they do involve emotional responses, critical discrimination, and judgment. Good judges of opera and oils will come to pay attention to the right things. Aesthetic competence in field sports is the habitual ability to pay attention to the sensations and emotions generated by those activities and to critically respond appropriately. Just as a bird dog sorts out the various scents it encounters, so the sportsman sorts through the impressions received and competently focuses on those of greatest importance. This is not the canned variety of nature aesthetics found at scenic turnouts. Aesthetic competence extends to the coordination of all one's senses, from the way the "air feels on the skin" when hunting to the push of the water when fishing. It has less to do with the cool appreciation of beauty than with one's performance in the activity, guided by paying close attention to the right things. Aesthetic competence is hard to pin down, but it is clearly of central concern to many who write about field sports. Indeed, it is sometimes taken to be the defining feature of these activities. Psychologically, some have written about the sense of "flow" and unity that occurs at times in such performances, that intensity of experience one remembers long after the events.

So how are we to educate for aesthetic competence? As we've seen in the last section, one answer considered, and, I think, ultimately rejected as insufficient by Leopold, is through more formal education. Indeed, Leopold devotes several essays to the role of formal education in conservation and bringing about a land ethic. He seems to be of two minds about such education: done right it can do wonders but done poorly, as he believes it usually is, it can continue to distance us from the land.[21] He asserts that, in addition to formal education, "nature study" may

> . . . lead to the development of the perception of natural processes by which the land and the living things upon it have achieved their characteristic forms (evolution) and by which they maintain their existence (ecology). That thing called 'nature study,' despite the shiver it brings to the spines of the elect, constitutes the first embryonic groping of the mass-mind toward perception.[22]

Nature study, as well as the activities of growing roses or birding, forms a part of field sports because the activities demand it. Leopold believes that nature study has the capacity to correct the course of conservation education, but we must avoid the view that natural beauty is merely the visually attractive or "pretty." The scenic and picturesque rely on culturally determined standards as to what nature "should" look like. Similarly, beauty as designed by humans in nature parks, zoos, and hunting preserves is artificially beautiful.

Aesthetic competence includes the use of all senses, not just vision, and relies on an appreciation of the environmental awareness of ecology and evolution of the land. Such competence is developed by immersion in the food chains and other connections linking the biotic community together. When aesthetic competence is added to the environmental awareness of the processes at work in evolution and ecology, and an ecological conscience to the shaping of desires and emotions, perception is promoted in the broadest sense. Leopold thus places a tremendous burden on the development of perception. To be perceptive in this systemic way is to acquire an understanding of ecology and evolution, and to habitually or "internally" desire harmony.[23]

Leopold, in his essay "Conservation Esthetic," defines some stages or aesthetic components of outdoor recreation. They range from a childish need to collect trophies as proof of overcoming and possession, through the need to feel isolated in nature, up to developing a refined perception of natural objects.[24] For Leopold, the issue is how to refine these feelings and needs, to move from the stages at which they have settled to higher stages of perception or environmental character. This refinement starts early in the education of youth. The excitement of a first fish or first shot can be intense and needs to be channeled or sublimated into growth. Aesthetic competence deals with our emotions and feeling: how do we address these? We can learn much from the examples Leopold uses in his writing. His method in much of his writing is to point things out to his readers, things he has perceived during his outdoor recreation and other wanderings. We are instructed in how to begin to see the world in this way during our outdoor pursuits. Whether he is describing tracking rabbits, hunting grouse, or sawing firewood for winter, Leopold is attempting to bring his readers to a high level of environmental awareness of the connections inherent in the communities in which he is participating—to develop in his readers a sense of the values of such biotic relations and evoke the right emotional responses to the intricacies described. When conjoined, these environmental virtues may unite in a true biotic perception. Perception is not merely seeing but educated discernment.[25]

Conclusion

We now know that there are three virtues defining the character of the sportsman, the possession of which will tend to preserve the biotic community. These are an ecological conscience, an environmental awareness, and aesthetic competence. The development of each of these requires the application of practical reasoning in a setting where there is a search for excellence. As such, the general biotic perception is the embodiment of practical reasoning, resulting in correct actions in hunting and angling and generally in the realm of the biotic community. This is the character needed to solve environmental problems faced by not just hunters and anglers, but also private landowners and environmental professionals. Contributing to biotic perception is environmental awareness, that knowledge of the connections between the species in various food chains and their locations, among other kinds of background knowledge. This is the knowledge of insect life and stream conditions sought by trout anglers; the knowledge of native plants and growth patterns valued by deer hunters. Also, there are the moral habits of sportsmen collectively referred to as ecological conscience. This conscience is reflected in the respect, care, and humility that require that one feel the right emotions for the biotic community. And finally, there is the virtue of aesthetic competence, which focuses the senses on the salient features of the biotic community and one's responses to them. Of course these virtues are variably instantiated in actual hunters and anglers.

It is important to remember as we proceed that these virtues are developed in a long educational process. The sportsman thesis, historically stated in its barest form, leaves this process out, and simply claims that field sports develop virtues. While some work remains to be done in refining our understanding of these virtues, the thesis, as I would state it now, holds that field sports, when envisioned as activities of practical reason devoted to excellence and the biotic good, are capable *in the long term* of developing the virtues I've identified. This educational process requires both the good will of the participant in choosing the activities for excellence and the mentoring of perceptive sportsmen.

Part Three
Problems for the Sportsman Thesis

There are several serious philosophical objections to the approach I have taken, which need to be addressed before the revised sportsman thesis is accepted. They will be the subject of Part Three. By answering these objections, I will develop a code for field sports, based upon the virtues already identified with alterations required to meet the objections. The first objection is one that occurs almost immediately to critics of field sports: aren't the same virtues also developed by activities other than field sports? Answering this objection will require a deeper exploration of the particular recipe for field sports. The second objection attacks the use of "sport" in "sportsmanship." It seeks to use the concept of sport against field sports, to show that they are elitist and, unlike "subsistence hunting and fishing," not morally acceptable. Answering this objection will afford us the opportunity to establish the centrality of the environmental virtues in all varieties of hunting and fishing. Finally, codes of ethics related to the sportsman thesis have been criticized both for their self-serving nature and their lack of consistency. These points will require that a new code be articulated consistent with the view of field sports already developed.

It is worth noting that these three objections are common to nearly all animal rights and welfare critiques of field sports. Once they are answered the disputes between defenders of field sports and their critics amount to a theoretical debate between various approaches to ethical thinking. I have maintained that virtue ethics provides an adequate basis for the sportsman thesis; this is my theoretical background. I have not engaged the theoretical foundations of other views because that is not the goal of this work.

Chapter Seven: The Substitution Problem

The substitution problem is one that must be solved if my argument in the past chapters is to remain viable. It challenges the very core of my view in that it accepts that hunting and angling might generate virtues, even the very ones I've articulated, but asks why one should pursue them in field sports when other non-lethal substitute activities can do the same thing. That is, granting that hunting and angling might generate environmental awareness, an ecological conscience, and aesthetic competence, surely other activities may do so as well, for instance, nature restoration projects, nature photography, birding, or gardening. And, since there seems to be a moral taint associated with field sports, based perhaps on issues of killing and cruelty, why, this objection concludes, continue in these activities when ethically equivalent substitutes are readily available?

There is a temptation simply to dismiss this objection on the grounds that it assumes a moral standard—killing animals is wrong—not accepted by the view I am defending. That is, one might argue that if field sports are indeed capable of developing virtue in the way I've outlined, then that is sufficient for their justification as instances of activities endorsed by a virtue ethics. Then the issue becomes a theoretical one of deciding between competing ethical viewpoints, a matter I do not address. But I believe there is value in making clear the actual differences between field sports and other similar activities in terms of the environmental virtues I've outlined.

In what follows, gardening and wildlife photography will be contrasted with field sports. One benefit of this approach will be a clearer understanding of environmental virtues and how they depend crucially on the experiences one has in acquiring them. By looking at gardening, an activity historically connected with virtue development, we will be forced to explore an important distinction between environmental awareness of what is domestic and what is wild. Contrasting wildlife photography with field sports will sharpen our understanding of what it means to develop an aesthetic competence and general biotic perception.[1]

Gardening and Field Sports

Vegetable gardening is an activity one might expect to yield the same environmental virtues as field sports because food is the goal and it can be done as a leisure activity inclined to virtue development and excellence. It is also an activity that rewards skill and practical reasoning. Surely the trio of virtues developed previously seem common to both field sports and gardening. An awareness of natural processes and food chains is enabled. An ecologically shaped conscience reflected in habitual care and respect for natural settings is characteristic of both good gardeners and good sportsmen. And one's aesthetic competence is focused on biotic conditions. Yet in hunting and angling, one kills animals intentionally. If the virtues generated are the same, and if virtue generation in the context of the biotic good is going to be the ethical justification of field sports, why not grow a garden instead?[2]

Others have offered some relevant answers to this question. Jon Jensen argues that both the *setting for* and *experiences had* in field sports differ significantly from those of gardening.[3] Field sports, he says, are specifically connected to the setting of wild communities, whereas gardening is connected to domestic ones. Also, in field sports, we experience the "cycle of life" by way of the killing and consuming of animals, and this blood connection is not established in gardening. This is confirmed by Michael Pollan, who writes about both gardening and hunting as pursuits of local, responsibly obtained food. Pollan, an expert gardener, goes hunting to experience, at least once, the uninterrupted chain of events that results in having meat on the table.[4]

These answers are correct up to a point. Field sports do take place in more or less different settings than vegetable gardening— sometimes wild settings. This, of course, needs qualification because gardening also requires a relationship with wild things, especially those wild critters intent upon eating one's produce. It is additionally true that the settings may overlap and intermix. In some parts of the world, hunting takes place in carefully landscaped fields, indistinguishable from gardens. And, of course, there is plenty of non-wild city fishing that goes on. Also, some hunters involve themselves in a kind of wild gardening or habitat development to encourage the population increase of desired animals.[5]

And yet, again, the *experiences* do seem very different in field sports and gardening. The gardener's experience and awareness is concerned with animals insofar as they harm or benefit the crops grown. Bees and cabbage worms, raccoons and deer are part of gardening, but they are an incidental, sometimes annoying, concern. The sportsman, on the other hand, is concerned with plants only insofar as they influence and provide clues about the flourishing of game animals. There is often in field sports an intense focus by hunters and anglers on the species they seek. So the hunter might desire to hunt as opposed to garden because of the wild settings and experiences. But is all this sufficient to answer the substitution problem? More importantly, can we account for these and other differences in terms of the environmental virtues identified?

Both gardening and field sports are activities of practical reason. They involve a set of skills together with a degree of background knowledge. They each require a special focus on features relevant to the task at hand in the face of factors of chance and uncertainty. Yet in each area of practical reasoning, there are clear contrasts between gardening and field sports. For instance, consider expertise in gardening. Even though there is really no linguistic equivalent to "having a green thumb" in field sports, the standard of an expert performing tasks effortlessly is common to both. Pollan, in *Second Nature: A Gardener's Education,* says:

> The green thumb gardener is the gardener who can nimbly walk
> the line between the dangers of over and undercultivation, between
> pushing nature too far and giving her too much ground.[6]

This image of balance or of walking a line between extremes is also, as we've seen, true of the environmental virtues generated by hunting and angling. I've explained those related virtues in terms of balance and harmony. The gardener with the green thumb achieves this balance in both his ecological conscience and in his environmental awareness. In addition to the dangers of over and under cultivation, there are the cognitive extremes of a kind of anthropomorphic mysticism on the one hand and an overly scientific approach on the other. As Pollan says:

> Observe the green thumb at work for a while and you'll notice
> how, in keeping with his preference for experience over abstraction,
> he approaches nature more like an artist than a scientist or engineer.[7]

Scientific knowledge may be helpful, but it is balanced against one's experience.

While both the gardener and the sportsman may seek this expert balance of practical wisdom, the skills needed are really quite different. For the angler, as we've seen, the skills are things like casting, reading the water, together with background knowledge about insects and food chains. Some anglers approach their activity armed with solar-lunar tables, weather predictions, and the latest scientific evidence on what fish can smell. Others simply go out and cast around for that feeling of being in the "good place" of a mystical union with the fish. What the "green thumb" anglers seek is an artistic balance between these extremes, the judicious use of science and insight always tempered by actual experience.

So gardening and field sports have the goal of expertise in common. Both the gardener and the sportsman become practically wise in doing the right things at the right time. Having a green thumb is the name for practical wisdom in gardening, whereas, for a sportsman there is that sense of being in "the zone," when one correct action seamlessly follows another. However we label them, these are both activities of practical reason. But that does not allow one to be substituted for the other. They do both generate habits basic to environmental virtues, but the specific habits formed, the background knowledge necessary, and the actions reached as a result of one's focus in each are distinct because of the different features they find important.

Martha Nussbaum has distinguished the general name of a virtue like "courage" or "moderation" from the "sphere of grounding experiences" to which the term applies.[8] The sphere of grounding experience is expanded or contracted by what humans find to be of importance or salient at a particular time and place. An ecological conscience, for instance, like the more generally recognized virtues of restraint and moderation, applies to different spheres of grounding experiences. The salient features in a gardener's experience, as indicated above, are different from those of an angler or a hunter, yet both sets of experiences are relevant to the development of an ecological conscience. The perception of gardeners and sportsmen are tuned to different stations and so the actions, which flow from the virtues, are informed by different inputs.

The experiences had in field sports mostly take place in non-domestic settings, as we've noted. I hesitate to call these places "wild" because of the notorious problems associated with this term. I don't believe we need to stop here to sort through these problems since it is at least the case that hunting and angling take place within food chains and biotic communities that are *relatively* free of human influence. Gardening, on the other hand, cultivates produce in a more domestic setting.[9] Vegetable gardening is an art of production wherein the product is comparable to making a pot or carving a statue. Field sports are arts of acquisition where the animals one acquires are there (mostly) by virtue of other (wild) food chains.

The biotic communities are different and so therefore is the kind of perception generated by each. The vocabulary of natural signs in gardening includes wilt and leek moths, but not rise forms and scat.

The perception of what is salient for each is different. Gardeners have their eyes and other senses focused on different things than sportsmen. Leopold, in one of his less charitable passages says:

> *The deer hunter habitually watches the next bend; the duck hunter watches the skyline; the bird hunter watches the dog; the non-hunter does not watch.*[10]

He's right about the way hunters watch but wrong about non-hunters, especially if those are gardeners. They watch too, just not the same things. (Leopold would be happy to agree with this, as he also is willing to credit the perception of birders, trackers, and even the unified vision of the ecologist who needs to perceive in all these ways.) My point here is that gardening promotes a perception different from that promoted by field sports. And these salient features fill out the spheres of experience differently.

As a gardener and an angler, perhaps I can use my own experiences to illustrate this point. When I am walking around the garden with my critical eyes on, I see insects that fall into three categories, even though they all part of the biotic community centered upon the garden. They are harmful, beneficial, or irrelevant. That cabbage moth is harmful, that honey bee is welcome, and that mayfly is irrelevant. These insects are part of the biotic community of my garden and are there because of their relations with the plants and animals in the garden and the surrounding area. My eyes are focused by the awareness I have of this community, limited though it is. I can track these relations through knowledge of the soil, plants, and weather. My angler eyes are quite different. Now the mayfly looms in importance; it is a Hendrickson, size twelve. How are the fish rising? In a leisurely roll or a panicked splash? Do I tie on a dry, nymph, or an emerger? These eyes are informed by knowledge of a different biotic community of streams, insects, and fish. I am equally focused in both gardening and angling, but what is salient to the activity is different. Environmental awareness is generated by both activities, but the content of that awareness is very different.[11]

Once we recognize that there is a great difference in the perception of sportsmen and gardeners, something no one would deny, we must also accept a difference in both the ecological conscience and needed background knowledge, which are both nourished by this awareness. In the first instance, one's ecological conscience is that virtue whereby one balances one's self interests against the good of the biotic community. But the biotic community that we are aware of makes a great difference here. It would be best to be concerned with both the wild and domestic—to both garden and hunt or fish—but the one is certainly not substitutable for the other.[12] Also, environmental awareness is equally necessary for gardeners and sportsmen but, again, the content is very different. For the gardener such knowledge includes not just the qualities and requirements of the produce, but also the right rotation of crops, the presence of birds, and quality of the compost. For the sportsman, the background knowledge is quite different.

So gardening is not substitutable for field sports because, even though general environmental virtues are present in each, the ingredients in the recipe for perceptiveness are quite different. The environmental character of the sportsman is not that of the gardener. And if we were to sample both, we'd quickly discover that they taste quite different.

It is, of course, still open to the critic to argue that these differences are not sufficient to persuade them and others that the flavor recommended by the sportsman's environmental virtues are sufficiently important to endorse them. While this will be taken up in Chapter Ten, it is at least clear now that gardening cannot be substituted for field sports.

Wildlife Photography

Wildlife photography is a wonderfully challenging activity often pursued in wild settings, by contrast with gardening. It sometimes requires the awareness of an ecologist and the tracking skills of a guide, together with all of the skills necessary for photography. It may fully engage one's ability to read natural signs. It is a potent source of environmental virtue, both moral and intellectual, because of the care for wild places and the knowledge required for getting close to the subjects. Critics of field sports, mistakenly conflating hunting with use of a firearm, quickly fasten on wildlife photography as an ethical alternative because the camera is imagined to take the place of the firearm. Both "shoot" at a target that may or may not be "captured" depending upon the skill of the operator. Wildlife photography seems to provide the perfect substitute for field sports for those who likely have experienced neither.[13]

Like that irascible hunter-philosopher Ortega y Gasset, we might initially be incensed by the suggestion that wildlife photography replace hunting. He says,

> One can refuse to hunt, but if one hunts one has to accept certain ultimate requirements, without which the reality 'hunting' evaporates. . . . The animal's behavior is wholly inspired by the conviction that his life is at stake, and if it figures out that this is a complete fiction, that it is only a matter of taking his picture, the hunt becomes a farce, and its specific tension evaporates.[14]

There are several elements in this quote worth noting. First, hunting and fishing certainly do have elements *not* present in photography, and one of those is the attempt to acquire the animal, i.e., actually get possession of it and not just its image. If this important "ultimate requirement" is not present, Ortega asserts, nothing else will substitute. Also, Ortega's use of "fiction" and "farce" emphasize the participatory experiences of field sports and the emotions one feels as one performs. Thus the "specific tension," which is not present in wildlife photography, is that cluster of emotions and critical responses one experiences in the process of hunting and fishing.[15] On the other hand, Ortega's speculations about the behavior of animals if they "figure out" they are not being hunted is surely itself a fiction.

Now critics of field sports—those suggesting a substitute—will, of course, acknowledge *this* point: field sports do involve the acquisition of animals sometimes by killing. But since the virtues generated appear to be the same in field sports and wildlife photography, why not hunt and fish with a camera? Is the perception any less acute? Is the awareness less sharp? Looked at in this way, Ortega's outraged comments are less convincing. We need to find out what the "ultimate requirements" of field sports mean emotionally and what our critical responses should be.

The contrast between the experience of acquiring an animal and the experience of taking a picture is also directly addressed by Jensen:

> Is there something special about the actual process of killing an animal that instills environmental virtues? Are there virtues associated with the kill in addition to the virtues of the hunt, or is killing simply incidental to the process of hunting?[16]

Jensen answers these questions in an interesting and relevant way. First, he argues, as we've seen, that field sports establish connections to *wild* communities. This coincides with our conclusion reached above. Jensen includes in his list of the virtues of hunting one he calls "connectedness." He says, "when a person hunts, kills, cleans, and processes the animal, the connections are deep and meaningful." This virtue "solidifies an understanding of our ultimate dependence on nature that is necessary for a proper humility."[17] So, in field sports, the *objects* of the connection, i.e., wild animals, and the *intensity* of the connection make real our knowledge of the ways we depend on nature. Jensen, in this context, mentions a common observation of many hunters and anglers: the intense memories they have of the *places* in which they have killed an animal or caught a fish. Ortega also elaborates on the heightened state of alertness experienced by hunters. And Leopold often mentions the permanence of the memories had in hunting and fishing. Jensen attributes this to the "depth" or intensity of the experience of killing an animal.

The critical challenge presented by wildlife photography as a substitute for field sports lies both in the seemingly common skill set needed to track and get close to animals and the environmental background knowledge necessary for successfully getting the chance one wants. Wildlife photography may require an environmental awareness of wild biotic communities and may generate the respect and restraint characteristic of the ecological conscience. As we've seen, others have tried to draw the line between these activities by emphasizing the "ultimate requirements" of field sports and the depth and intensity of the emotional experiences in field sports as compared to wildlife photography. These answers are right in presenting the experience of acquiring the animal as salient, but they fail to provide an explanation of the role of these experiences in virtue development. Wildlife photography is clearly more remote and less visceral than field sports as regards the acquisition of animals. The different quality of one's experiences in wildlife photography as compared to field sports is determined by the way one's focus or perceptiveness interacts with the other environmental virtues.

Imagine an angler wading in the river together with a friend who is a photographer. The friend's role is to get a picture of a fish just as it takes the angler's fly. They both know how to approach the fish, and they can read the natural signs with equal facility. They are both concerned about the quality of the water and the health of the biotic community in which they practice their arts. They go down the same path for a long way together. But the photographer's path diverges at a point where the angler continues on. The angler actually acquires the fish. To capture the animal involves not only those skills necessary to find it and get near it, but also those skills needed to acquire it. One's focus as an angler is on features that are relevant to this acquisition. Once the fish is acquired, the angler can kill it and prepare it for dinner or hold it up for his friend to take a picture and then release it. The perception of sportsmen is different subsequent to the event of capture as well. In field sports, there is in addition to the sight, other modes of perception, including the actual tactile capture of the wild animal and the tastes and smell of the food it becomes. This is a rich perceptual experience. It is more intense and nuanced in field sports than in close competitors like wildlife photography.

The image of the animal, as captured by the photographer, is open to manipulation, so its meaning depends upon the historical and social context into which is it introduced.[18] Excellence in wildlife photography requires seeing, focus, and framing. The salient features involved are composition, the use of light, and the interest of the action captured. An animal isn't *captured* by wildlife photography, rather an image is *created*, one that can then be manipulated to do what the artist wants: tell a story, shock, inform, etc. Getting the picture as a photographer is the means to doing something with it.

The mistake made by those proposing wildlife photography as a substitute for field sports is twofold. First, the emotional content and salient features are clearly different. Second, underlying this objection is the false assumption that the goal of field sports is satisfied by "shooting" the animal. But this, as we will see, is only a means for acquiring an animal when the actual goals of field sports are significantly more complicated.

Conclusion

Wildlife photography, gardening, and field sports are all practices or arts that "renew contacts" with nature, to borrow a phrase from Leopold. There are plenty of others, but they need not concern us yet. The substitution problem asks why hunt or fish when the same virtues are available from doing other less objectionable activities? The answer to this question is that while *some* of the same virtues (broadly speaking) may be generated there are several aspects of field sports that are unique. First, as regards gardening, the environmental awareness of wild communities is different from that of domesticated ones. Second, the emotional content informing one's aesthetic competence habituated by field sports goes well beyond that had in wildlife photography. These differences have allowed us to define field sports in a way that includes acquiring animals but does not make killing the only purpose of field sports. Killing is a *means* in hunting for the acquisition of some goods. The acquisition of virtue is as important as the acquisition of the *animal* as food for those who participate in field sports. A good of wildlife photography is the photograph obtained. It may be of great beauty and enduring value. The goods of (vegetable) gardening are foods, but they are acquired not from the wild but from the domestic cultivation of the soil.

Chapter Eight: Sport Hunting and Fishing

The problem we face in this chapter does not arise from a comparison of hunting and angling to non-lethal competing activities like gardening or wildlife photography, but rather from apparent ethical contrasts within and between various kinds of hunting and fishing. It is common for critics of field sports to contrast subsistence, sport, and commercial hunting and fishing, frequently with no further explanation, and to single out sport hunting and fishing for condemnation. Of course, economic writers discuss the "sport hunting industry" and states pass regulations on "sport fishing." This way of dividing things up doesn't do too much harm; we do need some way of categorizing these activities. The critical confusion arises when these economic or legal categories are taken to mark *ethical* boundaries. The framers of the sportsman thesis were, ironically, initially responsible for this ethical boundary drawing by elevating those who hunt for "sport" above those who hunt for "the pot" or for money. As we've seen, sport hunting and fishing were thought to be activities whereby one could hope to gain the virtues necessary to become a gentleman. Excluded from this elite group were women, indigenous peoples, and many other ethnic groups. The original appeal of the sportsman thesis was a hoped for social status recognizing the virtues gained by hunting and fishing for "sport" as opposed to for the more pedestrian needs of food or money.

Critics of field sports point to exactly this suspicious ethical elevation of field sports. For example, C. Mallory says this:

> . . . the point of the 'good sportsmanship,' which Leopold
> advocates is not to convey respect for one's prey as is commonly

argued by defenders of hunting, but rather serves to refine one's skills in a 'gentlemanly' fashion. This marks hunting as largely an elite activity practiced mainly by those with privileged cultural and economic status possessed by Leopold as well as the majority of hunters in North America.[1]

Because of this phony privileged status, some philosophical critics claim that field sports are actually immoral and should be legally banned *because* they kill animals for "sport," whereas subsistence hunting is morally sanctioned because such people *need* to hunt to survive.[2] These critics argue, in this neat inversion of values, that the hunting and fishing done "for sport" in field sports is simply unnecessary today.[3] These relatively affluent hunters and anglers, so the criticism goes, don't need the food and thus they are participating in "blood sports" merely for the sake of sport. This explains the often cited survey result that people morally approve "hunting for food" but disapprove "hunting for sport."[4] So, the exclusivity and elitism in the original sportsman thesis as a way of defending hunting and angling has now become the target of those who are critical of these activities. But since it is "*sport* hunting and angling" that are subject to moral disapproval by critics and moral approval by defenders of the original sportsman thesis, we should try to see what, if anything, sets field sports apart from other varieties.[5]

Hunting Defined

In order to define the role of acquiring animals in field sports, sometimes by killing them, we need a suitable definition of hunting that includes fishing as one kind of hunting. That this is important can be seen by briefly looking at one reductive and ultimately misleading characterization of hunting in general. Some critics simply define hunting and fishing as kinds of killing. For example:

> *"[t]o hunt . . . is to seek, pursue or otherwise locate animals, presumably those that are authentically wild,* with the object of taking their lives."[6]

According to this, the objective or goal of field sports as kinds of hunting is the killing of wild animals. But isn't it decidedly odd to portray the object as the piling up of dead bodies? Why should the object of hunting in general be animal killing, rather than something else for which the killing or capturing is the means? There is no doubt that most hunting *does* involve killing. The issue is whether killing is the goal or defining purpose of hunting. But, as we'll see, it's a mistake to assert that killing is the goal because this leaves unanswered the question of what purpose the killing serves. Surely this purpose must be to acquire a material good as in other acquisitive arts. Killing is one means of attaining this. The "hunting is killing of wild animals" definition is, thus, incomplete. It is incomplete because hunting is a way to acquire *some material goods* by the acquisition of wild animals.

Hunting and fishing, then, as human arts of acquisition, are ways to acquire wild animals for some human good. And, those who participate in *field sports, as kinds of hunting and fishing, seek the development of environmental virtue in addition to the good of the acquisition of wild animals.* Thus definitions that simply define hunting as intentionally "killing wild animals" mistake a means, i.e., killing, for the end, which is to acquire some goods. Killing is one means for the acquisition of these goods, never the end.[7]

Why is this characterization better than the bare "intentionally killing wild animals" account? First, in an extensive literature written by and about hunters and anglers, there are frequent declarations to the effect that field sports involve much *more* than killing.[8] While some believe that these writers are self-deluded, it seems much more likely that they are saying what they believe to be true. Second, it would simply be evil, as Theodore Vitali remarks: to "will the loss of life for . . . the sake of the loss of life . . ."[9] This bloodthirsty view of "man the hunter" has rightly been rejected by nearly everyone.[10]

Hunting (including fishing, as one kind of hunting) is the process whereby wild animals are acquired for some good. Participants in field sports do acquire wild animals as material goods but *also* seek to acquire the environmental virtues, which are themselves goods and serve the goal of the health of the biotic community. There are thus two goods sought in field sports. The virtues I've identified as available to participants in field sports are not elitist in the same way the "manly virtues" are in the original sportsman thesis. The environmental virtues I've discussed have up to this point been associated with field sports, yet as virtues they are clearly human capacities that might be extended to others. If gardeners and wildlife photographers share these virtues, surely other hunters and fishers may also.

Any ethical differences between sport, subsistence, and market hunting and fishing must be measured by a consideration of the biotic good. These labels are often used by critics as if their meanings and morality were completely clear. But at best, they may be thought of as three nests of participant motives, the strands of which often are wound together. Less prosaically, hunters and anglers choose to participate in hunting or fishing for a wide range of overlapping motives. To simply assume that "for sport," "for survival," or "for money" mark ethically significant categories is at best misleading and at worst a flat fallacy. Matters are much more complex than these simple labels suggest.

Subsistence Hunting

Subsistence hunting and fishing, the standard view goes, unlike field sports, are a matter of the survival of self, family, and community.

> *Subsistence hunting is the traditional practice, often imbued with religious significance, of habitually killing animals at a sustainable rate to feed one's self and family when no other adequate sources of protein are available.*[11]

It must be morally acceptable for a person to kill animals "to feed one's self and family," but this is not the case in field sports because "*sport* hunters hunt for the pleasure of the act; hunting is not necessary for them to survive."[12]

As should be clear by now, I believe that "the pleasure of the act" does not even begin to explain or define "sport hunting" any more than "hunting out of necessity to survive" explains or defines subsistence hunting.

Let us note first that if we were to accept survival as the morally relevant characteristic of subsistence hunting, the cases of justified subsistence hunting would be vanishingly few. After all, how many people's *survival* actually depends upon hunting? Perhaps the closest contemporary example might be Greenlanders, for whom the "gathering" part of "hunter-gatherer" is next to nil. But still, a critic could unsympathetically say, they might "survive" in other ways: state welfare or relocation. Also, the "subsistence as survival" view is so narrow that it distorts the activities of even textbook examples of hunter-gatherers, e.g., the Hadza of northern Tanzania. These people hunt, but also pirate the kills of other carnivores, and have access to a variety of plant food sources. They might "survive," although poorly, without hunting. The use of this narrow survival criterion is far too restrictive because it would imply that even many hunter-gatherers are not "morally exempt." This characterization also frankly insults the creativity of hunters and gatherers.[13] But if it is broadened by, for instance, including the survival of cultural traditions as a reason, it must morally allow for hunting and fishing justified by the acquisition of other external goods. For example, as Ted Kerasote has said of the Greenlanders:

> *If subsistence hunting was the only way, outside of welfare, to exist in the far north . . . why not also sell sealskins to make a little cash, which could buy people the few tools needed to hunt and enjoy some of the comforts southerners enjoy?*[14]

How does one establish that the Greenlanders are morally justified in eating seals but not in selling the skins?[15] Also it is likely that some Greenlanders find companionship or challenge in what they do. Does this then make them sport hunters?

Consider another example. When Lewis and Clark took their journeys they regularly hunted.[16] But on any given day their reasons for hunting included food, competition, protection, the collection of scientific specimens, and they often used meat to trade for other items. Their diverse and intertwined reasons for hunting were paralleled by the indigenous people they encountered. These people hunted for food, for trade, for ritual, and sometimes in competition. Since the goods derived from hunting are more or less the same, it is a mistake to assign some of these hunters to the class of sport hunters and others to the class of subsistence hunters based on some unverifiable attribution of motive.

One final example illustrates how mixed-up things actually are. Ice fishing is a popular activity in some places. It has its recreational aspects, but also allows some people to supplement a meager living by selling some of their catch. And the activity certainly adds food to the family table. Ice fishing is an activity that includes aspects of all three categories of subsistence, sport, and commercial.

A brief look at the origin of the concept of subsistence hunting and fishing provides additional evidence of its unsuitability as a morally exempt kind of activity. The origin of this concept may seem to be the anthropological distinction between hunter-gatherers and more agriculturally based groups. Then the hunter-gatherers become re-identified as subsistence hunters. But this cannot be right if descriptions of the rich complexity of hunter-gatherer cultures are to be believed. If the received view is that subsistence hunters do so "out of necessity" or as the "means of survival," this falsely warps the picture of hunter-gathers.[17] But once hunting is accepted as a richly textured component in their cultures, it is no longer very different from field sports as I understand them. The distinction between subsistence, sport, and market hunting owes its origin not to anthropological field research, but rather, as we know, to so-called "gentlemen" or "sporting" hunters themselves. The original distinction in this country was stated as that between sportsmen, pot hunters, and market hunters—which has some affinities to the older European distinction between hunters and poachers. Issues of race, class, and control are at the heart of the origins of the contemporary concepts of sport and subsistence hunting. Who had the right to hunt?[18] Who owned the wildlife? To bolster their case, hunters with aristocratic leanings sought to devalue what they called pot or subsistence hunting and to control market hunting. On this view, subsistence hunters are not the hunter-gatherers mentioned before, but anyone whose economic and social situation requires that their diets be significantly supplemented by hunted game. Field sports, by contrast, were seen as a way of developing character, an appreciation for wilderness, and a relief from the pressures of the business life. The irony is clear. Some aristocratically inclined hunters sought to elevate and morally distinguish themselves from others by means of this social distinction; yet now the self-imposed category of sport hunting is what draws fire from moral critics. Again, the problem is not that there are no sociological or economic distinctions, but rather the moral distinctiveness of such categories.

Subsistence hunting and fishing therefore are not *morally* distinct. Any such attempt to make them so is only initially plausible by restricting subsistence hunting to the motive of bare survival. In this way it is distinguished from other hunting in a morally relevant way. Yet once hunting and fishing are seen as historically complex and sophisticated, it is no longer possible to enforce a moral distinction.

The result of this is that there really is no viable *ethical* distinction between subsistence hunting and fishing, on the one hand, and that done "for sport," on the other. There are, of course, differing motives for participating in hunting and fishing activities.[19] These motives might include "getting some food," "building my status in my community," "winning a competition," "having a good time with my friends," and so on. Because these motives are so variable and easily changed, subject to one's age and context, they can't be used to morally appraise hunting and fishing as activities. To speak of "field sports" is strictly incorrect because this phrase only determines that more or less distinct group of hunters and anglers whose motives are *both* the material goods of the animals sought and *the environmental character development envisioned as an end*. I've previously referred to these participants as "sportsmen" and will continue to do so. But these virtues, as I've argued, are explained by the overarching good of the biotic community. The tendency of practices to preserve the integrity, stability, and beauty of this community is the ultimate standard for fishing, hunting, farming, logging, and all other related enterprises. This end *should* be used to ethically judge the various motives of all participants in hunting and fishing. The development of environmental character, as envisioned by the new sportsman thesis, is the distinguishing mark of sportsmen. The various motives and intentions of other people must, likewise, be evaluated in terms of their tendency to preserve the biotic community. So, as we'll see in the next section, a desire for competition, sometimes mistakenly used as a defining characteristic of sport hunting and fishing must, itself, be measured by the good of character development.

Hunting and Fishing as Competitive Sports

My purpose in this section is to consider the claim that field sports may be morally corralled with other sports of the more familiar competitive breed. If field sports are sufficiently like football and hockey, where winners are rewarded by the achievement of victory, then they seem ripe for moral condemnation. I shall argue that just as the reduction of subsistence hunting to "survival" does not provide a morally relevant difference, so the reduction of field sports to winning a competition, also fails. There is, it should be noted, another meaning of "competition" relevant here. Hunters and fishermen may compete with one another in a cooperative way to increase the level of excellence they might attain. Such competition is a kind of training or skill habituation that results not in winners and losers but in the general raising of the standards for all sportsmen. By watching other fly anglers cast and fish, one sees the tremendous skill required, the hours of practice put in, and to attempt to achieve that level is a kind of competition good both for the community of anglers and one's own excellence.

An example that illustrates a misguided winning-a-victory-sports-model approach to defining sport hunting is the following:

> . . . *participating in competitive sports necessarily means attempting to defeat an opponent. In sport hunting, the opponent is the hunted animal, and victory means killing it.*[20]

In general, this description of sport hunting implies that the basic features of field sports are those held in common with other competitive sports. But, as we'll see, it is both false that the opponent is the hunted animal and also false that victory is achieved by killing it. What is going on here is this: Such critics first note correctly that in the playing of competitive sports, like tennis, one attempts to win by defeating an opponent. Second, they incorrectly infer, via the ambiguity and vagueness of the term "sport," that since field sports are "sports" they must be like tennis. This is incorrect because, as indicated, "sports" are not competitive only in this way. Rock climbing is a sport the goal of which may be "winning" something. But equally, it may be competitive in the community sense of attempting to achieve excellence. Third, these critics, relying on the mistaken idea of field sports as victory-competitive, wonder about who or what the opponent might be, and fasten on the animals hunted. (They are called "game" after all!) But, they say, this is immoral and unfair because animals don't choose to participate. So the criticism is really based on a simple equivocation on the term "sport." The second conjunct is false because, as argued in the last chapter, killing is not the goal of field sports. Some critics take matters one step further and say that we should "stop referring to hunting as a sport or as a form of amusement," as if the very term is offensive.[21] Even some defenders of field sports have decided to give up the term "sport." James Swan, for example, advocates dropping the word because of its "negative connotations."[22] Ted Kerasote and Holmes Rolston have made similar suggestions.[23]

Defenders of the classical sportsman thesis have themselves again been partially responsible for this mistaken picture. For instance, Ortega y Gasset states the differences between subsistence (or, in his terms, "utilitarian") hunting and sport hunting this way:

> *In utilitarian hunting the true aim of the hunter, what he seeks and values, is the death of the animal. Everything else that he*

does before that is merely a means for achieving that end, which is its formal purpose. But in hunting as a sport this order of means to ends is reversed. To the sportsman the death of the game is not what interests him; that is not his purpose. What interested him is everything that he had to do to achieve that death—that is, the hunt. Therefore what was before only a means to an end is now an end in itself.[24]

This neat means-end reversal is intellectually appealing but must be resisted. For one thing, it misrepresents the subsistence motives in hunting and fishing by reducing them to the bare death of the animal. We've seen that this is a caricature. Ortega likewise gives a misleading impression of the "sportsman" when he says, "the death of the game is not what interests him." This makes it seem as if the animal acquired is not a good in field sports. This is surely incorrect; in field sports the animals acquired are goods every bit as much as the satisfactions of acquiring virtue. Ortega is right to emphasize that field sports are often seen as "ends in themselves" if, by this, he means they are pursued for virtue development as well as the good in the animals acquired. The bodies of animals are also necessary goods of field sports. If not, it is open for critics to wonder about the role of animals in field sports: are they merely "opponents to be defeated?"

There has been a semantic shift in the use of the term "sport" from the time of the creators of the sportsman thesis. Whereas early sportsmen wanted to distinguish themselves from people who *had* to hunt or fish, sportsmen are now saddled with "sport" as competition between them and the animals. The problem is the animals do not choose to participate in the activity. If the "opponent is the hunted animal," it would seem that the activity is a *fair* sport only if the animals somehow choose to participate (or, as in many cartoon versions, get to fight back.) In the absence of any evidence this is true, we seem to be led inevitably to the charge of unfairness in sport hunting.[25]

So how should we react to the many claims made about "sport" hunting and fishing? In my view, what is really indicated by this term is a rough and often misleading way of referring to a nest of motives individuals construct for themselves. This nest may include twigs from "subsistence" and "commercial" bushes too. Sorting the various strands of this nest into those that are ethical and those that are not is as improbable as it is unnecessary. What matters is that all varieties of hunting and fishing are practices intimately connected with the biotic community. As such, their activities and policies must be judged ethical or not by virtue of their tendency to preserve integrity, stability, and beauty of that community.

The Continuum of Hunting and Fishing

I have been unable to find any sharp lines separating field sports from other kinds of hunting and fishing. Neither the contrast with hunting and fishing for survival nor similarities with other competitive sports are sufficient for this purpose. But we cannot leave the matter here. We need some way of understanding the relations between various motives for hunting and fishing even though we cannot rely on the standard categories of subsistence, sport, and commercial. To do this we need to recognize two things. First, since there are no absolute distinctions available, the best we can hope for is a graded scale of activities based on the motives of participants. Second, the land ethic is designed to guide not just field sports but all practices of conservation. These include those who are motivated by commercial or competitive values. As such, the range of motives being compared will, I think, run from one extreme of engaging in activities solely for the sake of external rewards such as money and food, to, at the other extreme, the personal quest for virtue and internal reward. We must remember that even at the virtue-quest-extreme animals are acquired and they are always external goods. There can be no transcendental purity in field sports no matter how many fish are released.

Participants in field sports have been pulled in both directions. Some emphasize the internal rewards of virtue generation. Others, given the appeal of fishing tournaments and big-game hunting shows, have been pulled in the direction of the external rewards of winning competitions or other honors. Fishing for virtue doesn't require releasing the fish: we can both do something for its own sake *and* for the sake of a good meal. On the other hand, fishing to win a professional bass fishing tournament is typically dominated by the desire to gain some external reward and as such virtue development is hindered. These external rewards of competitions do not differ noticeably from the monetary rewards gained by selling one's catch, even though professional bass anglers may *also* be in it because it is fun. These are choices we make regarding our activities. One day is different from the next. The person who one day fishes commercially may not the next. Subsistence, sport, and commercial are not categories of people, but rather of choices people make. Participating in field sports, so I want to argue, is a choice of those motives that emphasize the quest for environmental virtue, all the while knowing that one will also eat or use the animals acquired. Ethical evaluation comes not from one's chosen attitude but from the guidance of the land ethic. Is what we are doing also the right thing for the biotic community, that is, *our* community broadened to include the land? This is where the ethical judgment can be made for all practices of conservation.

Consider several cases. In fox hunting as typically practiced in the United States, a group of well-heeled equestrians ride cross country after a pack of dogs chasing a fox. The acquisition of the fox takes place when it is "bayed" by the dogs so it dares not move. This elaborate affair takes place accompanied by fancy clothes, good food and drink, and an abundance of good manners. For most participants, this activity likely tends toward the virtue quest end of the spectrum, but really who knows?

At the other extreme we might pause to consider the rather popular television show, "The Most Dangerous Catch," which tracks the lives of crab fishermen and rewards them by the cumulative weight of crabs their boats can bring to dock. This is an interesting combination of factors. There's the money earned from the sale of the crabs, but there is also the competition between the "teams" on different boats. All the external rewards are here: money, fame, and honor. (The music is pretty cool too.)

Now based on the little I've said, can we make any ethical judgments regarding these activities? From one point of view, fox hunting is castigated because it allows foxes to be chased around for "no purpose."[26] From another point of view, it's the crab fishing that comes out the worse because the fishermen are "raping the oceans" for mere money and fame. (Well, really, I've never heard this objection—but it could be made.) Clearly we need some standard that will apply to both cases. Since they are both "practices of conservation" insofar as their existence relies on the continued diversity of biotic communities, we can ask about the ways they tend to preserve the biotic community, its integrity, stability, and beauty. Just as field sports have been evaluated in this way, it is possible to look at other activities.[27]

As another example, consider catch-and-release fishing. After one catches a fish one has the option (usually) to release it. This may be done in many cases without any lasting harm to the fish. This practice has become almost a religious tenet for some anglers: they release every fish. But some anglers and others see a problem with this decision. For example, the angler and philosopher A. A. Luce says "To hook trout and put them back into the water, unless they are too small to keep and quite uninjured, is to inflict pain, however small the amount, unnecessarily, and it therefore comes under the definition of cruelty."[28] More recently, John McPhee says, "I'm a meat fisherman. I think it is immoral to not eat a fish you jerk around the river with a steel barb through its mouth. I see no other justification for doing so."[29] This ongoing internecine conflict between anglers clearly illustrates a healthy ethical debate in field sports.[30] This debate is complicated by the legal designations of some waters as catch and release only, size limits, and attempts at species control. For instance, in some states certain fish must be released, e.g., sturgeon, and in others some species must be kept, e.g., brook trout in some cut-throat streams. These policies promote increases in the population for certain fish species.

But the fact that Luce, McPhee, and others see "no other justification" for fishing but getting food doesn't make it so. Food is not the sole "justification" for field sports. For the sportsman, the justification for field sports comes in the form of the virtues developed and the values placed on those virtues by society at large *in addition to* the material good of the animals acquired. The provision of food is important for the connections it establishes between hunters and anglers and the biotic community in which they practice their art. Sportsmen who release the fish they catch have, it must be admitted, acquired the fish and also perhaps the attendant virtues. They certainly may have a fully realized ecological conscience, which urges them to restrain their desire for food or trophy in favor of an improved fishery. They may have an intimate environmental awareness of the ecosystem connections necessary for the flourishing of the fish they release. They may be highly perceptive of the aesthetic depth of their experience, save one: they don't eat the fish. Anyway, catch-and-release fishing is not a kind of fishing any more than barbeque is a kind of cow. It is something one decides after the act of acquisition.

Field sports then are not really "kinds" of hunting but rather choices people make in participating in hunting and fishing. It was once acceptable to call people "sports" and even now we still recognize "good sports." Perhaps we can now see "field sports" as those people who tend to seek out the virtue-quest end of the continuum, while at the other extreme we find those who participate solely for the external goods of money or honor. Somewhere in the center are those who seriously desire the meat but also recognize the value of ritual and tradition. But regardless of one's motivations, the practice one is engaged in is to be judged by the biotic good.

Conclusion

The past two chapters have discussed problems for the upgraded sportsman thesis. There is first the possibility of substituting other non-lethal outdoor activities for hunting and angling with no net loss of virtue development. Gardening develops an ecological conscience, although in a more domestic setting than field sports, and wildlife photography certainly expands one's environmental awareness. But the actual experiences informing one's biotic perception are distinguishing elements including the killing of the animal, the food one eats as a result, etc. Leopold, in his essay "Conservation Esthetic," discusses the kinds of experiences one might hope to have outdoors and their values. This collection of experiences and their effects on how one perceives the biotic community is what makes field sports unique.

In this chapter, the ways field sports differ from other kinds of hunting and fishing became an issue because the usual categories of subsistence, sport, and commercial are so misleading. This problem is partially the responsibility of the original exclusivity of the sportsman thesis. It historically claims that "sport hunting and fishing" are both different from and better than other kinds of hunting and fishing primarily because of their power to generate virtue. This problem can only be resolved by expanding the scope of the sportsman thesis such that the good of the biotic community it endorses becomes the standard for all hunting and fishing, whatever the motives of the participants. As such, it is really no longer only *sportsmen* participating in field sports for their own sakes that fall under the requirements of this good. On the contrary, this good must guide every practice of conservation. The virtues inculcated by participants in field sports are explicitly designed to reflect the central doctrines of the land ethic. Thus field sports are at one end of a continuum where these virtues are sought.

Chapter Nine: A Code for Field Sports

Participants in field sports are characterized by their quest for excellences or virtues in the service of the biotic good. They also must recognize the good of acquiring the animal as essential. To what extent are these goals reflected in codes of ethics and conduct frequently cited and criticized? Such codes are endlessly reproduced in the sporting press and have become, in some ways, mere boilerplate. They should, in fact, state our highest aspirations for excellence, guide young people toward the land ethic, and provide rules of thumb to resolve some thorny issues within field sports. A code's usefulness depends on the intended audience. For those with lots of experience, it may serve as a reminder to keep them on track. For beginners, it provides rules that, if habitually followed, will help inculcate virtues. For non-hunters and anglers, it is part of the public face of field sports and, as such, may look like mere propaganda and deception.

Indeed, hunting codes in particular and sporting codes in general are at times mere propaganda. For example, if a high school discovers that some of the members of its football team are drinking alcohol, even if it is already against the rules, they may promulgate a new code, which they then ask football players and parents to sign. Similarly, when a hunting and fishing magazine decides that their sales and subscriptions will benefit, they may claim to support a code and then explicitly promote the idea that their subscribers are code-bound as well. This use of codes is often a cynical attempt to manipulate public perceptions of these activities.

In this chapter I shall discuss and answer some serious objections to the significance and coherence of sporting codes in field sports. Then, keeping these criticisms in mind, I will propose a code consistent with the environmental virtues specified by the sportsman thesis.[1]

The Trouble with Codes

Some have argued that sporting codes are just irrelevant when it comes to the morality of field sports because the practices they are codes for are immoral anyway. Thus codes are merely a kind of public camouflage that shields hunters and anglers from what they actually do and make their actions appear acceptable to themselves and others. Also, it has been claimed that sporting codes are internally inconsistent or self-contradictory. Let's look at these objections as a way of guiding the discussion.

One critic says:

> *Labeling something an "ethic" in the sense of being a code for conducting oneself, such as "the hunting ethic," does not establish that it is a code of moral values or even that it has moral significance. The moral value of hunting remains an open question, even though hunting has long had an "ethic."*[2]

The answer to this objection, given the argument of the previous chapters, is roughly this: If a code can be made consistent with those environmental virtues derived from the land ethic, and the land ethic is a version of a broadly accepted ethical theory, i.e., Aristotelian virtue ethics, then it must have moral significance. That is, the sportsman thesis asserts that environmental virtues are inculcated by field sports. This thesis is justified by its alignment with environmental virtue ethics in particular and virtue ethics in general. However, to make good on this answer, any code for field sports must really *be* based on the environmental virtues identified.

Some feminist critics of field sports attack the sportsman thesis directly. One says her goal is

> . . . to lay to rest the ethic of the 'good sportsman,' as well as any notion that hunting may provide a sound conceptual 'resource' for an environmental ethic, or any ethic at all.[3]

One could hardly find a clearer rejection of the sportsman thesis. I want to argue, after all, that field sports *do* provide a resource for the development of certain virtues foundational to the land ethic. This critic explains her objection by saying that hunting ethics and codes are "camouflage" for the real nature of hunting. She says:

> . . . hunters employ ethical discourse as a means of shielding the hunter from the actual experience of the animal he kills, and as a means of renouncing personal responsibility. The focus of the hunter is on his own interior mental state. As long as his mental attitude is said to conform to a particular ethical code, his violent behavior is thought to be legitimized.[4]

If I understand this correctly, what happens when we hunt and fish is this: we kill animals, which should make us feel guilty. But, we convince ourselves that we've done nothing wrong, because we've followed a code of good sportsmanship. Thus, in our own minds, we are not guilty of an immoral action but rather innocent because the code says so.

The only way this objection might seem legitimate is if one has already decided that field sports are immoral. Then *any* attempt to justify them must be wrong, and so those who attempt to do so are simply deluded. Even though the objection assumes what it wants to prove, it does point to a real problem. Sportsman codes, as I've said, are everywhere.

There's little attempt on the part of their creators or publishers to ever justify the various rules cited. Without such justification it is completely understandable that people not familiar with field sports would see codes as mere camouflage.[5]

Yet another objection is that hunter ethics are "paradoxical" because

> . . . hunters become more ethical by hunting in a way that is sensitive to the animal's interests in avoiding pain and continuing to live; nevertheless, this very sensitivity and respect for animals entails that hunting is not justifiable, that even true sportsmen are not acting ethically.[6]

The objection is that there is a conflict between those elements of a code that require, for example, "clean kills," which seem to take into considerations the individual "animal's interests" in continued life and avoiding pain and yet, inconsistently, violating those interests by killing the animal. This objection is answered, as we'll see, by emphasizing that a code for field sports is *only* paradoxical if it must endorse rights for individual animals. But the code for field sports developed in this chapter is suitably "holistic" and thus not subject to this criticism.

Evaluating a Code for Field Sports

Once these problems with field sports codes are stated, our next step is to evaluate some of the particular recommendations made by existing codes. The contents of field sports codes historically vary according to which region, state, or nation one examines. However, many existing codes are sufficiently general to provide us with a place to begin.[7] Given the objections stated above, the environmental virtues of an ecological conscience, environmental awareness, and an aesthetic competence, will be used to evaluate the content of a widely distributed code of conduct. This process will reveal any changes and additions needed to the code.

What follows is a long quote from "Be a Responsible and Ethical Hunter," a section of *Today's Hunter,* which is the manual used for hunter education classes in New York and many other states.[8] Even though this code is written for hunters, it is clearly applicable to fishermen as well.

The Hunter's Ethical Code

Aldo Leopold, the 'father of wildlife management,' said, 'ethical behavior is doing the right thing when no one else is watching—even if the wrong thing is legal.'[9]

The ethical code hunters use today has been developed by sportsmen over time. Most hunting organizations agree that responsible hunters do the following.

Respect Natural Resources

Leave the land better than you found it.

Support wildlife conservation programs.

Adhere to fair chase rules.

Know your capabilities and limitations as a marksman, stay within your effective range, and strive to improve your skills and the likelihood of a clean kill.

Ensure that meat and usable parts are not wasted.

Treat both game and non-game animals ethically.

Abide by game laws and regulations.

Cooperate with conservation officers.

Report all game violations.

Respect Other Hunters

. . .

Respect Landowners

. . .

Respect Non-Hunters

Transport animals discreetly—don't display them.

Keep firearms out of sight.

Refrain from taking graphic photographs of the kill and from vividly describing the kill within earshot of non-hunters.

Maintain a presentable appearance while on the street—no bloody or dirty clothing.

I've included most of the code from *Today's Hunter*, with the exception of those clauses referring in detail to one's relations with landowners and other hunters. The parts I have included are of most interest both from the point of view of the sportsman thesis and also those critics mentioned above. This code is clearly organized around the various "interest groups," whose tacit or explicit acceptance is desired by hunters and anglers. To those with a critical philosophical eye, this code will appear ethically mysterious and to some extent duplicitous. The rules or clauses of the code, while certainly sensible, are opaque as to their justification. Respect for "Non-Hunters" seems more public relations than ethics. Some elements of this code concern mere legality and, while these are clearly important, a code surely must go beyond them in its requirements.

It is important to keep in mind that codes are merely lists of rules, and rules are always general. Specific guidance must be supplied by what we've previously discussed as practical reason. We need to act in ways that are appropriate to the conditions in which we find ourselves. That is why virtues—permanent dispositions—are crucial. These are practiced responses to similar situations. A code, as a list of rules of thumb, only hints at this complexity. Codes thus can offer guidance, but the hard decisions and actions in the field are the results of practical reason precisely applied.

There are several clauses in the above code that stand out as of immediate ethical interest. When we are asked generally to respect "natural resources," what does this entail beyond "supporting conservation programs" and sighting in one's firearm? When the code asks us to leave the land (and water) "better than we found it," is this an implicit acknowledgement of the centrality of the land ethic? This would provide an ethical basis for the "respect" demanded by this code beyond the public image-enhancement of a clean, legal, non-bloody sportsmen.

The environmental virtues inculcated by field sports should provide justifications for the central components of any such code. First, reflecting on the role of an ecological conscience, there should be guidance provided regarding ethical issues of restraint, respect, and moderation in actions and emotions. This requires a critical look at the doctrine of fair chase mentioned in the above code. Second, an adequate code for field sports must advocate the accumulation of knowledge of the whole biotic community, as required by environmental awareness. Third, the rule to "ensure that the meat is not wasted," must be seen in the context of bringing responsible food to the table. Such experiences connect us to the biotic community. Fourth, a code must advocate the hands-on involvement of civic husbandry barely hinted at with the bland injunction to "support conservation programs." Finally, the various clauses in the code must not only set minimum conditions for compliance but must also include the highest standards of excellence available. That is, a code must reflect the progression from beginners to those seeking mastery in the activity. These philosophical points will justify certain rules of sporting codes but, practically, must remain in the background, lest codes turn into philosophical treatises.

Excellence and Fair Chase

One's character, ecological or not, is a living thing; it grows as we do and as it does it is nourished by experience. We must then imagine the slow growth of the excellences of character from youth to adulthood. A code, on the other hand, is a set of rules and recommendations without awareness of age and development. As such, the code above, like many others, is set at a minimal level: be safe, obey the law, etc. But, as we know, there is an expectation of eventual excellence in field sports. This is what drives the sportsman forward toward the refinement of perception. So codes must somehow state minimal conditions for beginners and at the same time urge sportsmen to climb the ladder toward excellence.

The environmental virtues promote moderation, knowledge, and taste in the realm of environmental matters. Leopold notes that it is the "peculiar virtue" of these that "the hunter ordinarily has no gallery to applaud or disapprove of his conduct. Whatever his acts, they are dictated by his own conscience. . . ."[10] This relative isolation places the burden for developing these virtues squarely on the sportsman. Sportsmen who develop these are willing to restrain themselves in the face of many temptations—for example, to shoot at animals too distant, to use gadgets that replace skill, to shoot a sitting bird, etc. —with "no gallery" present. Anglers are similarly tempted. Habitually showing such restraint is a mark of excellence. If one has *respect* for the biotic community then one will show *restraint* in these ways.

So why should hunters and anglers bother to actually *follow* these rules if no one is watching? This is one source of the objection mentioned above that codes are not "morally significant." Without a good answer to this question, less charitable critics are more than willing to jump in with their own answers, like self-delusion or camouflage. Rules about respect—so prominent in the Sportsman Code above—need to be grounded in the environmental virtues if this objection is to be met. The rules in a code must be used by mentors to guide beginners in the long and difficult process of developing habits or "instincts" that come to form an environmental character.

Consider the recommendation to "follow rules of fair chase." The history of these rules is closely tied to the history of the sportsman thesis. It made sense in the past because one key element of the sportsman thesis was that gentlemen should show restraint and moderation when hunting or angling. This was the original, rather limited idea of conservation. Once this justification eroded, however, the doctrine was transformed into a summary of the rules in the "sport" of hunting or fishing. It seems to offer a normative guide for those who hunt or fish for "sport," just as the rules of tennis guide that sport. Jim Posewitz says:

> *Fundamental to ethical hunting is the idea of fair chase. This concept addresses the balance between the hunter and the hunted. It is a balance that allows hunters to occasionally succeed while animals generally avoid being taken.*"[11]

Fairness here is determined in part by giving game animals a fair chance to escape. Unfortunately, as Posewitz clearly recognizes, this injunction is not sufficient to the purpose of making field sports ethically acceptable to critics. The reason we must go "beyond fair chase" (as in the title of his book) is that the once acceptable explanation for being fair, that is being a gentleman, will not serve today. Nor, as we've seen, does it make sense to say that fair chase rules are like the rules of any game or sport. Fair chase needs to be explained in terms of the environmental virtues and the good of the biotic community. In particular it needs to be understood as a habit following from the inculcation of environmental virtues.

The rules of fair chase typically include a limit on advantages for the hunter or angler, the self-imposition of rules such as to only shoot at birds when they are flying, or those properly worked by the dog, or not to keep female salmon yet to spawn, or even a strict catch-and-release commitment. These self-imposed rules make the acquisition of an animal more difficult and hence increase the role of skill. The rules of fair chase thus should be understood as invitations and reminders to increase one's level of skill excellence, a never-ending process.

One might object at this point that surely there are plenty of highly skilled sportsmen who are also ethically challenged. I guess we have all met those who are masters of their crafts but are still jerks. Perhaps

Leopold or Roosevelt each had highly attuned environmental virtues. Yet in other areas of their lives they were less than conscientious. This is all true, but not germane, because my claim is much more circumscribed. All I want to claim is that in the realm of environmental matters, a pursuit of skillfulness in field sports will inculcate that quest for excellence so necessary for virtue development. So to show restraint as a sportsman is a matter of habits formed.

The pursuit of skillfulness is exactly the element in field sports that is both the impetus for, and proof of, environmental virtue. The restraint shown by following a rule of fair chase is really a demonstration of skills: the ability to find and pursue animals with minimal technical advantage, for example. Fair chase as a method of pursuit that allows animals the chance to escape is increased by lessening dependence on finders and gadgets and by improving one's own skills of observation and movement. Similarly, respect shown by "not wasting meat" is developed and demonstrated by developing one's culinary skills so delicious meals may be prepared with the meat. One shows respect for landowners by developing skills of friendly interaction. A code is necessary to remind beginners and their teachers of these skills of restraint, but these only become real habits of excellence once expertise is established by skillful performance.

So respect as a rule in a code really means that a host of skills of restraint must be developed. For the beginner, these rules are a reminder. For the expert, they are tools for teaching. To the non-sporting public, they need to be explained at every available opportunity. As such, perhaps the first clause in our modified code should simply read: Sportsmen should continually develop their skills in the quest for excellence.

The Biotic Good and Holism

So far in our discussion, the code for field sports has required only explanation and revision. However, at this point we'll need to make an addition to the code, because the biotic good—from which the environmental virtues are derived—has yet to find a role. According to the code above, hunters should "learn more about the habits and habitats of game and nongame wildlife and their management needs." While we can certainly agree with this, hunters and anglers will ask why they should do this. What explains this line of the code? Part of the justification might be self-interested in that the more we know, the better our chances of acquiring an animal. But how do we motivate the "universal curiosity of the land mechanism" that Leopold recommends, awareness of the vast web of ecological relations that must be present for any species of animal to exist at all. Again, this may be a matter of seeing the difference between beginners and experts. As young people develop their skills in field sports, they will also begin to develop that awareness of natural signs signaling the presence of quarry. This gathering of the meanings of natural signs will continue if nurtured and rewarded until it becomes a mature mastery of ecology and evolution. Field sports must promote access to the evolution and ecology of the biotic community as a whole, two concepts which receive almost no attention in *Today's Hunter*. This is so important, yet so under appreciated by merely suggesting one "learn more about wildlife."[12]

In conjunction with this awareness, we must also come to the realization of how little we actually understand of this ecological process. Leopold puts the matter this way:

> *The last word in ignorance is the man who says of an animal or plant: 'What good is it?' If the land mechanism as a whole is good, then every part is good, whether we understand it or not. If the biota, in the course of aeons, has built something we like but do not understand, then who but a fool would discard seemingly useless parts? To keep every cog and wheel is the first precaution of intelligent tinkering.*[13]

Environmental awareness in field sports must be aggressively holistic, i.e., such knowledge must be systemic and unbounded. But this also requires humility, because to attempt to be aware of the biotic community as a whole is also to be aware of our deep ignorance about many of the relations and elements that make up this community. The object of our awareness is the "land mechanism" as a whole, and the proper attitude to take is that of the "intelligent tinkerer." This attitude recognizes that we are mostly ignorant of the nature of the whole biotic mechanism and thus must be conservative in our actions and policies. We certainly don't know enough to simply remove portions of the community to satisfy economic or recreational needs. Leopold very likely has in mind predator elimination policies. Yet this "assumption of ecological ignorance" cannot paralyze us; we need to act if only to begin to undo some of the damage already done.[14] We must act on knowledge that is both scientifically defensible and based on the precept that the land mechanism is a whole resulting from eons of evolution.

In codifying a holistic environmental awareness, we have also provided an answer to one of the challenges above. That challenge is that codes for field sports are "paradoxical" because they seem to embrace the interests of individual animals while at the same time denying these interests in the service of "sport." But a code for field sports need not and should not be individualistic in this way. What is required is an awareness of the biotic community as a whole. The cogs and wheels referred to by Leopold are not individuals, but species and the various ecological relations required for their continuance. Field sports codes have innocently but unwisely used the language of individuals. But this needs to change. Field sports codes need to be stated holistically. As such, this portion of the code should require that we keep learning about the biotic community within which we practice field sports, and that we judge our practices by the good of this community.

Local Food, Responsibly Acquired

It is becoming increasingly apparent that it is important for all of us to take responsibility for the food chains in which we participate, whether these involve factory farms and shipping containers or backyard gardens and local trout. This requirement follows from both our knowledge of the biotic whole and an ecological conscience attuned to the connections between human flourishing and material conditions. In the case of sportsmen, the requirement is an even higher calling because in field sports the body of the animal acquired must always be valued for the good it is. As such, the food chain that we participate in by acquiring that animal becomes of concern as well.

Aesthetic competence has been discussed previously as the capacity we develop to select, refine, and appreciate the experiences we have in field sports. What is important in these experiences, as in other aesthetic areas, is that we value them for their own sakes and not only for any other good obtained. That is, we come to appreciate the trout we catch not only for the food it will provide but also for its biotic connections and for the lasting impressions its acquisition makes on us. The virtue of aesthetic competence keeps us oriented toward the inherent value of the experiences, in addition to the obvious practical value of the food. We are asked to develop our aesthetic appreciation of our experiences of connectedness with the biotic community. This perception for the sportsman is irrevocably situated in a particular place and time. Aesthetic competence grows over time from the youthful appreciation of the colors and behaviors of game animals as objects to a perception of the beauty of the biotic community responsible for those features.

Consider the rule above that requires that sportsmen "ensure that meat and usable parts are not wasted." This rule is religiously followed by many, but its justification is unclear. It is not simply a matter of the "clean plate" mentality. Rather, the messy process of turning animals into food is aesthetically rich, full of emotions and smells, tastes and sights. The aesthetics of field sports is a full aesthetic experience, one that completes the chain from the biotic community to the sportsman. (In contrast, the completion of this chain is interrupted for the wildlife photographer.) Completing this chain is a matter of certain skill development. *Today's Hunter* contains sections on butchering and safely storing animals for consumption. It could logically also contain recipes for the preparation of meals using acquired animals.

My point here is simply that responsibly eating wild animals means making them more than just a meal; eating wild animals is a celebration of the natural processes and personal experiences involved in having that meal. This emphasis on the quality of the experiences, perhaps captured by the retelling of stories, orients the participants toward their connections with the food chains in their biotic community. As such, these meals provide a standard by which others can be measured, not only for the culinary quality but also for the connection to the local food chain. This may account for the value placed by many sportsmen on local place and its connection to food.[15] Hunting and fishing are now and always have been an important part of the local foods movement. We find ourselves connected to a nearby stretch of river or that covert. Anglers sometimes mention their "home waters" with a kind of reverence. Unfortunately, advocacy for this local connection to food is absent in current sportsman codes.

Civic Virtue and Husbandry

The New York Sportsman code says we should support wildlife and habitat conservation: "Provide hands-on and financial support for conservation of game and non-game species and their habitats." This clause of the code encourages us to embrace what Leopold calls the "sense of husbandry . . . realized only when some art of management is applied to land by some person of perception."[16] We've just concluded that perceptive sportsmen have an intimate, full, and local sense of connection to the biotic community that surrounds them. The next stage in this development is naturally a sense of the social conditions necessary to preserve it.

At stake are those conditions necessary for field sports to continue to exist and even flourish. Every practice requires that certain social conditions be maintained for their continuance. From birding to bowling, there are necessary conditions for these activities to continue. In general, for field sports to continue, two conditions must be preserved: First, the health and diversity of the biotic community must be maintained, such that hunting and fishing never diminish this diversity but on the contrary enhance it. Second, the human community must be willing to embrace field sports. There must be public access, funding, a regulatory structure, and enforcement of game laws. These are matters sanctioned by society at large. If these conditions are not maintained, field sports will not survive. To the extent that sportsman behavior undermines these conditions, it is in violation of this rule. The mature development of civic virtues enable sportsmen to do whatever is in their power to improve these conditions. They must contribute to the overall health and diversity of the biotic community upon which their activity depends. And, they must contribute to the flourishing of their activities in the human communities in which they reside. We shall explore these civic responsibilities in Part Four.

Conclusion

Existing codes for field sports are in need of modification. They must be aligned with the development of environmental virtues, the biotic good, and a responsible attitude toward food. Only in this way can they meet the objections to their relevance and coherence. The modified code must make plain that achieving excellence requires the development of environmental virtues. Practicing the restraint of fair chase is part of this quest. Environmental awareness must also be deepened by requiring knowledge of the biotic community as a whole. For instance, practical knowledge about trout behavior must develop into a holistic knowledge of stream ecology. The person who is fully connected to the biotic community must become the model for beginners and others. This is accomplished by inviting young sportsmen to complete the chain of experience from finding and acquiring animals to their consumption as food. Finally, a set of civic virtues must be developed and collected under the label of husbandry if field sports are to retain their place in the public sphere.

It is important to note that the code I've sketched is no longer confined to sportsmanship, but has application to other practices of conservation. A code that requires environmental virtue, attention to the biotic good, and responsible food practices is as useful for commercial fishermen as for fly anglers. This generality shows that this code is not elitist. Neither is there any inconsistency or paradox in the code, because the unit of analysis is not the individual animal but rather species and their relations to the land.

Our revised code for field sports should read as follows:
1. Seek excellence.
2. Value the biotic community.
3. Take responsibility for food.
4. Practice husbandry.

Part Four
Implications for the Future of Field Sports

Though I've outlined a modified code for field sports and answered some important objections, there are several remaining issues of sufficient importance to warrant specific attention. In this part, I cover the future of field sports and what sportsmen must do to maintain a publicly and ethically acceptable basis for their activities. The recommendations made in the following chapters are in some ways radical, and will provoke howls of complaint from some hunters and anglers. Nevertheless, they are implied by the modified sportsman thesis and the code of conduct proposed in the last chapter.

The goal of Part Four, then, is to make some suggestions about what field sports must do to persist and perhaps even flourish. This means that various cultural and political forces must be slowed and reversed because they are damaging the prospects of the continued existence of field sports. As sportsmen, we need to address issues such as postings to exclude field sports on private lands; the trend toward hunting and fishing on exclusive vacations and at private ranches as alternatives to public spaces; the hyper-competitiveness of tournaments and the professionalization of field sports; the burgeoning use of gadgets; all terrain motor transport; firearms and hunting; policies of stocking fish and game; and the use of sportsmen as agents of wildlife management. All of these are hard issues, often left to economic calculations and personal preference. We need an alternate, an ethically based way of considering them that takes into account the environmental virtues and the code of conduct developed in the last chapter.

Besides putting our own house in order by modeling the best behavior, what can be done? The answer to this question is complex, and I will begin the task in two ways. First, I will explain how the desire to develop environmental virtues is thwarted by the forces of commercialization, competitions, and the over-reliance on gadgets. This explanation will not resolve these complex issues, but it will offer some much needed guidance. Second, I will suggest a partial answer lies in sportsman education for youths and conservation-group membership for adults.

In Chapter Ten, I connect environmental virtues to some other general standard values of outdoor recreation, civic values whose importance is sufficient to justify the continuation of field sports. These values will then be employed to evaluate various problems standing in the way of this continuation. Chapter Eleven examines a force that, if left unchecked, will ultimately undermine the capability of field sports to generate virtue. This is the force of commercialism and includes not only the economic power of the "sporting industry" but also the marketing of money tournaments and the portrayal of field sports in the media. In Chapter Twelve, necessary changes in sportsmen education programs are evaluated based on the criteria developed. Chapter Thirteen considers the judgments made by sportsmen about the value and meaning of game animals, given my account of environmental virtue, and contrasts this with a standard view taken by some state and federal agencies. Critics often fasten on these viewpoints because it looks to them like animals are merely live targets stocked for the "games" of field sports. What are game animals? What values should sportsmen find in game animals? Finally, in Chapter Fourteen, I look for areas of common interest between field sports and other kinds of outdoor recreation. Only in this way can we avoid the fragmentation and weakening of those activities best suited to develop environmental virtues.

Chapter Ten: Field Sports and Civic Virtue

As sportsmen develop environmental virtues with regard to conservation of the biotic good, they also become aware of threats to field sports. Threats presented by animal rights advocates are ethically based, often focusing on the potential cruelty of field sports. The view I present in the previous chapters is my answer to these critiques: if field sports are sources of environmental virtue, and virtue ethics is a well founded ethical theory, then field sports are ethically justified. Other even more serious threats to field sports, however, come not from these actual opponents, but rather from unexpected social and economic directions. As we shall see in the chapters that follow, the public image of field sports has, in many ways, been hijacked and co-opted by some of the very institutions and groups that claim to be friends and defenders. The poor public image of field sports is also very much enabled by the behavior of many hunters and anglers. If field sports are to be ethically justified in terms of virtue development for the biotic good, those forces tending to undermine this end must be exposed and opposed. And, most importantly, solutions and alternatives must be proposed.

Field sports have the power to develop an ecological character. This is a good thing for sportsmen and, if my argument is correct, good also for the biotic community. But, while having an ecological character is necessary for the justification of field sports, it is insufficient. The existence of a cadre of virtuous sportsman does not suffice by itself to modify the behavior of other participants in field sports. Personal "image enhancement" will not preserve the future of field sports. For example, when sportsmen, honestly or not, try to shield others from the actual nature of the practices of hunting and fishing, they are not addressing the central problem. The images of hunting and fishing portrayed in the public realm by forces of commercialization and competition have a power that overwhelms any "clean clothes, clean plate" campaign. One need only pick up any magazine devoted to field sports to see the problems: even when the articles assume that field sports are connected with some virtues, the advertisements for vacations, gadgets, and fast boats undercut this goal.

We need to be able to argue that those economic, political, and institutional goals moving field sports away from environmental virtue are wrong. And to do so, we need to state in plain terms how the virtues of field sports are being compromised. This may form the basis of public appreciation and, perhaps, continued acceptance of field sports.

Renewing the Standard of Excellence

Leisure activities play an important role in redirecting our conceptions of the good life, in remaking our pursuit of expertise and excellence. While these ideas might initially seem implausible, they have strong historical support. As we've seen, Aristotle held it to be true. More recently, Leopold supported the claim. Classical leisure activities are unimpeded and chosen for their own sakes; they are thought to be occasions of that perfect happiness sought by all. That is, during their performance, we experience that freedom and satisfaction often absent during impeded or other controlled activities. Of course, we need to keep in mind that not all "leisure activities" are such: shopping or playing video games are pale imitations of the more robust and skillful activities classically recognized as leisure.

Within this narrower conception of leisure, participants will wish to continue their activities in order to pursue the satisfactions derived from progress toward achieving excellence. In the case of field sports, there are two potential impediments to their continuation. First, the biotic community must be healthy enough to support the activities. Second, the civic community must see some value in field sports sufficient to allow for their continuation. As such, participants must act to maintain the right *social* conditions. If we like to fish, and clean water is required for us to do so, then we must insure that water quality is maintained and improved. Thus the health of the biotic community in which we wish to hunt and fish must be maintained. But also, the social and political environment must be conducive to these activities. For example, if we wish to hunt or fish, we will need public access to hunting and fishing places. We must therefore attempt to bring it about that there will continue to be such places. Since I've already discussed the first ecological point in some detail, I will here focus on the second.

Aristotle believes pursuing excellence in leisure is both a private and a *public good*. Since our capacity to live the good life depends not only on becoming virtuous people but also living in a state that sanctions these virtues, these are clearly connected. Put another way, no matter how environmentally virtuous we might individually become, our educational, economic, and political institutions also need to move in environmentally beneficial ways.[1] Field sports are not, contrary to comments made by Leopold himself, essentially private activities with only the "Almighty" watching; they must also conform to public opinion.[2] The image presented or represented to the public, means, in effect, that we have the citizenry in general watching over our shoulders. That is, excellence in the practice of field sports must be appreciated and valued by the non-sporting public if we desire these activities to persist let alone flourish.

In his essay "Wildlife in American Culture," Leopold says that "by common consent of thinking people, there are *cultural* values in the sports, customs, and experiences that renew contacts with wild things."[3] This "common consent" about the value of outdoor leisure activities has seriously eroded in the intervening years, to the point that the non-sporting public genuinely does wonder about the continued value of field sports. The continued viability of field sports depends on sportsmen and like-minded people reestablishing the centrality of their virtues in the public sphere. As I've mentioned, this is a political undertaking requiring an action plan well beyond my limited means. However, we might at least come to understand the problems in terms of the environmental virtues and the kind of excellence they entail.

Leopold identifies three values in outdoor sports, customs, and experiences. First, he mentions the traditions of woodcraft and hardiness of field sports, which he calls "split-rail value," meant to invoke a sense of the pioneering spirit. This is of value to society at large, he says, because it "reminds us of our distinctive national origins and evolution." Second, there is cultural value in activities that exercise the "ethical restraint" of sportsmanship. Third, there is value in experiences that remind us of "our dependency on the soil-plant-animal-man food chain." These are obviously connected to the environmental virtues I identify above, but here their role is not so much shaping the characters of sportsmen but in laying out the civic standards expected of field sports.[4] That is, the centrality of these and other values must be sanctioned and reaffirmed in the public realm. Only by this extension of the environmental virtues to the public realm can field sports be rescued from their current state of decline.

The problem with these values, as stated by Leopold, is that they appeal to a public attitude that may no longer exist. When Leopold points to split rail value, he is partially appealing to the ancient and now mostly severed connection between field sports and war fighting: those values of woodcraft and hardiness were central to the soldier as conceived in the middle of the twentieth century. Similarly, the smooth slide from sportsmanship to being a team player and good colleague has become rather bumpier given the troubles faced by professional and amateur sports. Even the human-land food chain connection is likely today seen as an anachronism. Who really wants to know where their food comes from? Ask any fifth-grader.

If the connections between these values and public acceptance have indeed been severed, we need a way to reconnect them. Or, perhaps better, we need a way to ground the environmental virtues I've identified in the public realm, to make the case for a public appreciation of the excellences of field sports. My approach is to show that these virtues are not just good for the individual and the biotic community, they are also still important in the public realm. As such, they are useful for the task of deciding some critically important public issues surrounding field sports. While, admittedly, this is not a fully developed civic grounding, it does go some way to arguing for the public role of sportsmen.

In the remaining sections of this chapter I will make some suggestions as to how the environmental virtues of sportsmen discussed above might be connected to broader civic concerns.

The Civic Value of Simplicity

The ecological conscience acts as a kind of moderation where the salient features of a situation are temptations to excess as opposed to restraint. Habits of restraint are a good thing in economic matters generally, if only because economic value always seems to trump other kinds, especially in decisions about land use. While we can never completely remove economic value from our decisions, it needs to be balanced by something else. This is especially true when we seem driven to acquire things simply for the sake of acquisition. In this context, surely activities that habituate restraint and moderation are welcome.

In "The Outlook for Farm Wildlife," Leopold says there are two opposing philosophies of farm life.

> 1. The farm is a food factory, *and the criterion of its success is salable products.*

> 2. The farm is a place to live. *The criterion of success is a harmonious balance between plants, animals, and people; between the domestic and the wild; between utility and beauty.*[5]

The contrast between these two views of farm life is a bit anachronistic; it has a nearly exact parallel in Aristotle's discussion in the *Politics* of the contrast between two perspectives on money, wealth, and their bearing on the good life. On the one hand, there is wealth as a means to provide necessary and useful things for the family, community, and life.[6] Unfortunately, Aristotle says, some people wrongly believe that

> "... *the whole idea of their lives is that they ought either to increase their money without limit, or at any rate not to lose it. The origin of this disposition in men is that they are intent upon living only, and not upon living well.* . . ."[7]

There is little difference between Leopold's farm for living and Aristotle's natural household management except that the latter expresses no concern for the *biotic* community. Even so, Aristotle is endorsing a life of moderation and restraint as the best life for individuals, as well as best for the community, because it is limited by what we can use and store. Each man's pursuit finds an end once one has enough to live.[8] The greed of solely pursuing wealth for its own sake has no end since money can be accumulated indefinitely. Both Leopold and Aristotle connect their concepts of restraint or moderation to the goal of living *well*, as opposed to merely living.[9]

If an ecological conscience is fundamentally a kind of restraint and moderation, then it becomes a limitation on acquisition, a counter to greed and avarice. And if these characteristics are of permanent value for our culture, then the people who develop this and the activities that aid in this development should be valued as well.

As such, it deserves to be valued as a civic virtue.

Some hunters and anglers understand that a good life is enabled by the pursuit of simplicity. Those meals and experiences in field sports become examples of a kind of uncomplicated happiness. Surely this is part of the appeal of both Izaak Walton and Thoreau. On those occasions when one can eat from the field and garden, one realizes that the other material things one has acquired or desired are of less importance. The "simple life" is frequently extolled by psychologists, anthropologists, and philosophers as the path to happiness. Leopold's "split rail" value can become a real alternative, that is, a real civic value, for others who don't hunt of fish.

Consider the "local food movement," which, I believe, shares many of the cultural values identified for field sports. Given that this movement enjoys public approval, and if, arguably, the values it endorses are consistent with those above for field sports, then by examining it we might better see why these values deserve to be publicly acknowledged.

The local food movement is surely complicated, and I'll leave it to others to map out the historical and social causes. Even the term "local" is variously defined by allowable geographical factors, but there is a belief that getting food locally is better for health of individuals, the biotic community, and the economy of the local human community. The food is grown, ideally, by people one knows, or, at least those within one's community, and the money becomes part of the local economy. Meat, produce, and dairy products are all finding their way into this system. Included in this belief is a desire for food that is safe and doesn't economically support "factory farms" of various sorts. As such, the movement has ethical, economic, and biotic components. But most importantly, it has an aesthetic component in the way is offers a unified vision of getting food to eat and its preparation and consumption.

The movement is old fashioned, or "split rail" in an admirable way: returning to traditional means of gathering food. When Michael Pollan enjoins us to return to the methods of our grandparents in how and what we eat, he is also appealing to tradition. The reason our ancestors split rails in the first place was to fence the livestock out of their crops and gardens. There is thus value in keeping alive traditions of food gathering. Hunting and fishing are also traditional ways of gathering food. There is nothing more local than a pan of brook trout or a steak of venison. And like the local food movement, there are other values derived from this tradition: ethical, economic, and biotic.

Ethically, the local food movement is motivated by an intense dislike and distrust of large-scale agriculture and meat production. This point is often made in ecological terms: the food production system is unsustainable in its reliance on fossil fuels, fertilizers, and unregulated waste disposal. These factors are important because members of the local food movement have developed a fine-turned ecological conscience, one that motivates them to find alternatives. By virtue of the same habits, some hunters and anglers find themselves opposing large-scale agriculture and factory farms, and for exactly the same reasons. Hunters and anglers are concerned also with biotic health, and it is their environmental characters that explain their stance.

The Civic Value of Connections

Field sports intimately confront us with our dependency and connections to the land and its biotic organization. We should be concerned that we are moving away from the land and so forgetting what supports us. Other activities such as birding, gardening, and wildlife photography go some way to making this connection, but in a manner different from field sports. The civic value of such experiences can only be seen when they are contrasted with the "nature deficit" suffered by many of our citizens and children.[10] I've often used a class exercise to illustrate this problem to my students. I'll ask them to trace the origin of some food they like. It quickly becomes apparent that most such foods—chips, health bars, beer—simply have for them no discernable origin in the land. I ask them to recall the last time they ate some food where they knew the exact origin, like a fish they caught, a mushroom they collected, or a grouse killed by a family member. They usually can't come up with a single item. I sometimes give out plantlets to grow for extra credit. An amazingly large number of students decline this opportunity because they simply know they can't grow a plant. Now, I don't need to argue that we as a society are disconnected from food chains. Others have made this case in great detail.[11] Field sports are of social value because they are one model for making these important connections.

A second, often overlooked, civic benefit of hunting and angling in this regard is that sportsmen spend a lot of time in careful observation of areas rarely visited by others. Remote mountain streams, backwater swamps, the thickest cedar clumps, and the wide ranges of dry lands are all under the perceptive eyes of hunters and anglers. Reports on the relative health of these areas routinely flow from these observers, together with alarms when they are being altered. Hunters and anglers are perceptive in the ecologically important way in that they can tell when things are not right; they can read the natural signs. This is again a civic service. I cannot overemphasize the importance of boots in the fields, streams, and lakes. In many cases, there is simply no other way to track the health and diversity of the land. These sportsmen are in it for the long term: they will hunt or fish in the same areas over decades and thus become the repositories of knowledge of the environmental state of the land.

Another cultural value is the political connections made by husbandry in environmental matters.[12] Many sportsmen are members of organizations such as Trout Unlimited, the Atlantic Salmon Federation,

The Ruffed Grouse Society, etc. These are national organizations with local chapters devoted to the solution of local issues, such as the control of invasive species, reforestation, clean water, and the removal of defunct dams. They are natural expansions for participants in field sports and indicate again sportsmen's civic character.

As a member of several of these organizations, what often strikes me is the good will displayed by members in discussing plans for action, even when they are poles apart on other political issues. These organizations serve a role that brings citizens together from all political persuasions in the pursuit of common environmental and conservation goals. This is surely a civic good, to have groups of people with local knowledge and a fierce drive to preserve the local biotic community join together for political action. Such organizations provide one of the key ways in which we can continue to educate both ourselves and others in the real goals of field sports. Others have recognized this crucial role. For example, O'Neill argues that "it is within the context of such practices that an appreciation of and concern for the goods of the natural world occurs."[13] There is a clear difference between these practices and membership in various organizations whose goals are merely lobbying and fundraising. The difference lies between giving money and consent to a group whose goals one supports and the shoulder-rubbing meetings and activities of local chapters of organizations. There is always a blend of these, but the activism of husbandry is only present to the extent that one is required to get one's hands dirty.

Conclusion

Leopold's three cultural values are revitalized by seeing the connections between environmental virtues and broader social concerns and movements. The simplicity of food gathering and preparation, the making of political and natural connections, are permanent aspects of the good life. As we'll see, they tend to subvert the roles of consumerism and its mindless pursuit and acquisition of wealth to the exclusion of other more enduring values associated with living the good life. They demand we be connected to our food and other products, especially when this has been blocked by inattention and commercial design.

Field sports have the capacity to alter the sportsman's conception of the good life. The sense of tradition, economic moderation, and restraint, and the powerful links to the biotic community are enlivened in the civic activism of sportsmen. These values must be socially promoted and publicly embodied by participants in field sports if they are to retain their importance. A serious challenge to the civic virtues of sportsmen is found in consumerism and political interests and their influence on field sports.

So far, these public values are little more than promissory notes. Their actual value must be found in the critical uses to which they are placed in the public realm. Put otherwise, the public may justly remain skeptical of field sports even give these promises. Surely this skepticism has two sources. First, the bad behavior of hunters and fishermen continually undermines any claim to virtue. Second, the image of field sports is contested even beyond this behavior: there are powerful interests at work, the goals of which are not virtue but profit and power.

Chapter Eleven: Money and Politics

Jim Posewitz, in his excellent little book *Inherit the Hunt,* concludes with a chapter titled "Finding Our Way in the Twenty-First Century." There he identifies many present and future dangers facing field sports. One clear danger is the "commerce of gadgets, hunting machinery, catered experiences, and fees for access to what is ours."[1] The "most ominous threat" is that field sports will be possible in the future only for those with sufficient wealth and thus "create the equivalent of a new royalty of the hunt in North America."[2] He adds that this threat is "compounded when public trustees yield to the concentrated influence of the minorities seeking privileged access to public resources."[3] Posewitz is dramatically right about these threats posed by commerce, politics, and privilege: they diminish public support for field sports insofar as they are perceived as the purview of the wealthy and therefore elitist. But, what is the ethical basis for opposing these forces of commerce and political special interests? Does the revised sportsman thesis have resources available to expose the flaws of these trends?

Posewitz recognizes that there is one all-important segment of American society that will decide the fate of field sports. These are the people who don't hunt or fish and really don't give it much thought. This covers a lot of people whose openness to field sports must be maintained. One argument they find compelling is the need to manage wildlife. As limited as it is, this argument finds acceptance because of wildlife-human conflicts, for example deer-car accidents. But field sports cannot be supported by this alone, because it just isn't true that the vast majority of wildlife populations are really controlled by field sports. Another argument employed in this context is the economic justification of field sports. Here it is the money made that counts. This money is derived from many sources: advertising, equipment sales, travel, television revenues, and fees. This argument, as commonplace as it is pernicious, must be rejected.

The ethical justification for field sports, if we accept the sportsman thesis, must ultimately rely on their effects on environmental character. But this requires that we critically examine current economic justifications, because some economic and political institutions tend to corrupt the ability of field sports to generate virtue at all. Participants in field sports must be motivated by the desire for excellence in addition to the acquisition of an animal if there is to be the possibility of environmental character development. Those selling technical shortcuts to the acquisition of animals co-opt this essential motive. The environmental awareness and perception generated by reading natural signs can be replaced easily by hiring guides and following the "hot spot" industry. The civic virtues required by participation in field sports are compromised and made unnecessary when hunting and fishing are pursued in private preserves made possible by individual fees and pay-to-play arrangements. Finally, those environmental virtues connecting us to the land are stretched to the breaking point by pricy sporting vacations in exotic locales as compared to the thick connective tissue built by years of local hunting and fishing.

Gadgets and Sporting Equipment

There are two problems we face in considering field sports gadgets. First, it is very hard to define what gadgets actually are. Surely field sports will require the use of *some* tools like firearms, rods, reels, lines, dogs, etc. How are these different from gadgets? Second, once we have a satisfactory answer to this, what are the actual problems with the use of these? What do we give up?

Sometimes, as an in-class exercise, I have my students look through some of the many catalogues I receive from hunting and fishing outlets such as Cabela's, Gander Mountain, and Orvis. My question for these students of outdoor recreation is to pick out things they consider "gadgets." They've read Leopold at this point in the semester and his view that ". . . there must be some limit beyond which money-bought aids to sport destroy the cultural value of sport."[4] They also know that I have managed, sometimes inadvertently, to acquire a lot of stuff, so there is the possibility of them picking out something I own. A lively discussion often ensues, especially when something is picked out that I consider essential, such as polarized sunglasses for stream fishing, that they consider a mere fashion accessory. We try to figure out what a gadget really is and what is really essential.

Sarah Pohl, in her article "Technology and the Wilderness Experience" argues that gadgets or "devices" as she calls them, can "skew and diminish characteristics unique to the wilderness experience, and these characteristics are necessary for exercising excellence in wilderness recreation."[5] That is, if the goal one has in hiking into the wilderness is, like in field sports, excellence, then one should be very careful about the technology one brings along. Pohl is not as clear as she might be on the actual reason excellence is impaired by gadgets, but I think she would agree with the view that skillfulness and mastery are necessary for excellence and devices that simply replace skill are obvious problems.[6] In this context, she uses a distinction between two kinds of technology, a "device" and a "thing."

> *A thing requires our skill, engagement, and practice; a device*
> *offers us instantaneous results, but fails to involve our engagement.*[7]

In field sports, rods, firearms, and bows are tools that do require skill, engagement, and practice. The use of each of these tools or "things" is open to evaluation and ranking from beginner to expert. There are fairly clear standards one can use to make these judgments. It is necessary to practice these skills often under the guidance of experts to become competent. Gadgets offer shortcuts to skill development. One example is the use of GPS to determine location as opposed to a map and compass. There are many cases that tend to confound this issue, but one thing is clear: it takes more practice to use a map and compass and there is a wider range from beginner to expert than in the case of GPS. If excellence is the goal, we might justly ask why take shortcuts?

Another example is that of using a shock collar for dog training. This device straps around a dog's neck and holds two electrodes up against the skin. These electrodes can remotely deliver a shock or, if adjusted to a low level, a mere tickle of the sort one of those old hand buzzers might give you. I once witnessed a misuse of one of these collars. This was a failure on the part of the dog owner at many levels. First, it occurred while hunting, and dog training should never occur while hunting, it takes place well before or after. Second, this guy seemed to think that his dog was something like a remote controlled drone that could simply be driven around. The dog was yelping from the shocks and the guy was screaming curses and pushing the button but no learning was going on at either end, except perhaps the dog was learning to look out when cursed. I mention this incident because I also have a shock collar and I've used it on my bird dog. It is a real short cut, and I'm not particularly proud of my purchase and use. In its defense, if the collar is used properly at the right time, it can save the dog from developing some vices such as deer chasing. This is what I cured with it, and it worked extremely well. But dogs have been trained without these gadgets for thousands of years. This case illustrates the temptations of gadgets or devices. Animal training is also a practice whose goal is excellence and that means not just excellence on the part of the dog or horse but excellence on the part of the trainer. The skill required can be diminished or even replaced by gadgets.

Shock collars are not the "things" mentioned above. They are not tools that engage us or require much skill. But other items that are part of the field sport experience are tools in this sense. A fly rod engages our desire for mastery, as does a shotgun. We are constantly reminded of our failures in the use of these: the backcast in the bush, the botched crossing shot, or the rueful and accusatory look of the dog for yet another miss.

While sportsmen deserve some blame for yielding to the temptations of gadgets, we must also realize they are subject to intensive and well-funded efforts to get them to so yield. Once we recognize gadgets for what they are, i.e., devices designed to replace skill and thus lower standards of excellence, we must make every effort to promote skill and excellence. We should always ask, while engaged in field sports, what are we doing? What is the goal of this? The economic argument in terms of money generated by field sports must always be amended to include the generation of virtue or else this ethical dimension is lost.

Competition and Field Sports

Posewitz points out the power of commercial interests as a serious challenge to the future of field sports. When one adds up the money to be made from ATV's, bass boats, television revenue from hunting and fishing shows, destination sporting lodges, and all the gadgets, one quickly becomes aware of the power of the sporting industry. Once opportunities for public field sports become squeezed by posting and private reserves, money will talk the loudest, and we'll be in danger of reverting to the past elitism and aristocracy of field sports. Insofar as field sports become privatized, civic virtues are diminished. This privatization of field sports is going on in destination hunting and fishing and the increasing use of private preserves for field sports. Just as gadgets subvert the core goal of excellence in field sports, so commercial interests co-opt the sportsman's role as citizen. There must be ethical considerations of sufficient weight to counteract the force of commerce. Let's see how this might work in a particular case.

I am lucky enough to live near a large cold-water lake. There are many opportunities for public access and recreation on this lake including sailing, fishing, wildfowl hunting, swimming, and many others. There is also money to be made from tourism. Recently, in addition to vacation dollars, we've experienced the economic benefits of a half-dozen professional bass fishing tournaments. The boosters for these tournaments cite national exposure for the region and money in the pockets for owners of motels, restaurants, and other service providers. The tournament organizers hope the weigh-ins will be attended by locals and the taped results watched on television. These tournaments have their own public relations people to place articles in the local papers and get coverage on the local news. The participants in the tournament get around the lake in bass boats with explosive speed matching their spectacular NASCAR colors. The winners of these tournaments are rewarded with a big check and as much publicity as possible.

Now there are a few curmudgeons around who are unhappy with this situation. But their muted complaints about unsuccessful catch-and-release policies and boat noise are met with stern economic warnings of loss of revenues and jobs. This economic wind blowing from the bass tournament boosters is withering. Can ethical considerations counteract this force? Can we be assured that these ethical arguments get some sort of a hearing in the public realm? Sportsmen must be willing to carry their ethical concern into the public arena. This is the power of civic virtue. It is easy to just let things go. But sportsmen bear a responsibility to speak for the biotic good. This must take into account economic factors, but also make clear that these are not the only things that count.

From the point of view of the sportsman thesis, the ethical problem with professional fishing tournaments is that they replace the central goal of virtue generation in field sports with that of winning external rewards. Field sports are capable of generating virtue because they are chosen for their own sakes. They are not means for garnering prize money. It is the possibility of choosing expertise and excellence as ends that aligns fishing with other virtue-generating forms of leisure. In these "professional" tournaments, fishing becomes a purely quantitative enterprise with weight, numbers, and dollars as the criteria of success. At the end of the tournament winners are declared. The goal is not fishing for its own sake but a prize or external reward. Commercial interests are also served. A sleek, fast bass boat is needed to get to those good spots on the lake first. A dozen rods are already rigged with market-ready lures for maximum casts with the right lure colors. Similarly, in hunting, one seemingly needs a camouflaged ATV to get you to the right spot and then drag the deer out. And you need the big truck to haul the ATV or bass boat. This is the goal commercial interests would like sportsmen to accept. But it takes them in the wrong direction, away from excellence measured in increased mastery instead of numbers or money, from reading natural signs instead of fish finders, from moving slowly through the biotic community instead of rapidly skimming over it.

It is the civic responsibility of sportsmen to call attention to this diversion. No one else will do it. The integrity of field sports is already sorely challenged and cannot be allowed to further disintegrate.

Sporting Vacations, Private Preserves, and Public Access

Catalogues for hunting and fishing gear now sell not just the gadgets but also the places to go. Exotic fishing locations and hunting safaris are for sale along with boats, ATV's, rods, and firearms. These locations are sometimes foreign but may also be private preserves closer to home. The common feature is that one must be willing to pay the price. If the price is high enough, one gets expert guides, five-star dining, and brandy with cigars after dinner. This is quite different from the kind of vacation one might take at the low end of the economic scale, a local camping trip combined with some fishing or hunting. There are many levels in-between as well.

From the point of view of the sportsman thesis, the problem with these pay-to-play experiences is not just that skillfulness is displaced by convenience, but that connections to the local biotic community are thin or none. Or, to be more precise, these connections while possible are fairly easy to avoid. On the other hand, some people do make strong connections to distant biotic communities by fishing or hunting experiences. Because some have had the opportunity to fish in some other parts of the world, they do have concern for these places. But their ability to practice actual husbandry is seriously challenged by distance. Local streams and coverts present no such barriers.

As more land is posted as off-limits to field sports, and as more land succumbs to other uses, the opportunities for field sports are diminished. This makes pay field sports all the more attractive. You can be sure your spot is reserved and there will be no hassles about access. But again, this is not a direction that will ensure traditional public access to field sports. That direction will only be assured by sportsmen engaged in discussions with public representatives and private landowners. The biotic community is held in trust by private landowners and the public. The biotic community is not a squatter on private lands, to be ejected when unwanted. It can be changed but not removed. If the sportsman thesis connects biotic good with good character, it is required of sportsmen to preserve this good by civic engagement and husbandry.

Working against this civic requirement on the part of sportsmen is a common error in thinking about the purpose and role of organizations to which sportsmen belong. In his article "Leisure and Democracy: Incompatible Ideals?," J. L. Hemingway points out that leisure activities and the groups they spawn are now often viewed as mere "lifestyle enclaves," which have three characteristics:

> . . . *leisure is linked with consumption; leisure is privatist, cutting the individual off from the public arena; and leisure is a search for reinforcement derived from being with those who are much like oneself.*[8]

But if I'm right, sporting groups must reject each of these. They must reject consumption and emphasize skill; they must embrace the public arena as determined by their civic virtues; and they must actively encourage diversity and connections with those of different political beliefs who are participants in field sports. Once this reorientation of organizations representing field sports is accomplished, they can no longer be accused of representing "special interests."[9]

Conclusion

For the sportsman thesis to maintain its viability, those forces that tend to subvert it must be exposed and opposed. In particular, the sporting industry, with its focus on competitions and exotic destinations, gadgets and luxury, must be seen as undermining the core commitments of sportsmen. The political influence of special interests such as those promoting tournaments should be tracked carefully for their potential damage to field sports.

Chapter Twelve: Sportsman Education

One example of the power of political special interests in field sports comes from a recent attempt in New York State to pass a bill exempting members of the military from taking the hunter-education class required to obtain a hunting license, an exemption already in place in several other states. The nine-hour hunter-education class culminates in an exam which, when passed, allows the participant to obtain a hunting license. The proposed bill would have allowed members of the military who are residents of the state to merely show their military ID to obtain a hunting license. The thinking is that people in the military routinely get training in firearm safety and thus do not need the course. Hunter educators countered that there is much more to hunter education than firearm safety, and thus even experts in firearms need the course. The bill was not passed, but it illustrates the way special interests may seek to influence the education of sportsmen in field sports, which is the topic of this chapter.

The sportsman thesis is a hypothesis about the education of character.[1] I've argued that an ecological conscience, environmental awareness, aesthetic competence, and certain related civic virtues are enabled by field sports. The development of these virtues requires significant practice because their full realization comes only with the knowledge, habits, and perception of an expert. Unfortunately, this idea of character education is often at odds with the policies and practices of actual sportsmen education courses attended by those who desire a hunting license.[2] My experience in this regard is as a hunting instructor in New York State but, given the countrywide use of the hunter education manual *Today's Hunter*, much of what I have to say will go for other states too.

Those who mentor young hunters and anglers face two problems, within either the confines of a course or outside in the field. First, virtues require for their inculcation significant periods of time; they must become habits, and habits are only formed after significant practice. Yet, the nine-hour hunter-education course is directed almost exclusively at getting students to remember some information about hunting, wildlife, and firearms that they then can rely on to pass the test. Where, we must ask, is the character education? Second, if the environmental virtues of ecological conscience, environmental awareness, and aesthetic competence are the defining internal goods of field sports, we must demand that the education of young hunters and anglers be designed to bring this about. Field sports are activities done for their own sakes; they are leisure activities. It is this central feature that allows us to think that they might be capable of generating environmental virtue in the first place by moving participants toward conservation. Yet this feature of field sports is undermined by the merely instrumental role as "tools of wildlife management" allotted to hunters and anglers by the state and federal institutions responsible for hunter education.

Character Education

Aristotle believes that three things contribute to the development of virtue: one's nature, habits, and habituation, and reason or speech.[3] Together these will contribute to the formation of one's character. Since we as educators can't do much about the *nature* of our students, we tend to concentrate on habituation and speech. In hunter education we especially focus on the giving of speeches: we *tell* students what they need to know to pass the test. We *explain* things they don't understand. But what can we do about their all-important moral habits?

One answer, which we hope is true, is that much of this part of character education takes place in the home under the guidance of family mentors and other adult role models. The course is just a licensing program after all. It can't take the place of the years of guidance necessary to form the characters of young sportsmen. But this answer doesn't jibe with the official goals of these courses. The International Hunter Education Association (IHEA), which "serves as the primary resource for information on hunter education," states that one of its goals in hunter education is to "cultivate honesty, self-discipline, self-reliance, responsible behavior, and good citizenship among hunters."[4] This is clearly a version of the sportsman thesis. It probably over-reaches in its august list of virtues, but more importantly, it leads us to ask where, in the curriculum of hunter education courses, this goal of character development is addressed. Some of the students who pass the course are likely able to memorize and recite these virtues, just as the Boy Scouts require that its participants are able to recite an even longer list of twelve virtues, but that is a far cry from actually *having* these virtues or any others.

It might be easier to simply pass off the hard work of habituation to family, friends, and teachers, but I also think this is a mistake. Sportsman education must reinforce and extend those good habits already present in young hunters and anglers and also try to correct those that tend toward vice.

The manual *Today's Hunter*, along with the sportsman educators who use this publication, does realize that virtue development is a long and arduous process:

> *The difference between the novice hunter and the true sportsman is wisdom, which is acquired by the experience gained from making decisions, acting on them, then seeing the consequences of your actions.*[5]

This is an honest recognition of the lifelong commitment necessary to become a "true sportsman." A nine-hour class for novices will be only the beginning of a long process, which may culminate in expertise, mastery, and wisdom. What can we do as hunter educators to facilitate this development?

One suggestion is to start early. Fishing, which has no course for licensing requirements, is hunting with a hook and line. The development of character begins early, and fishing is an excellent way to begin to inculcate those important environmental habits of character. Reading the water, awareness of biotic communities, skillfulness can all become aspects of character even before the age is reached to become a licensed hunter. These skills and habits can be developed by early walks and experiences detailed by many outdoor educators.[6]

Firearms Education

These nascent virtues in novices can be further developed if we can find a way to reallocate the time we have in hunter education courses.

There is one glaring problem that, if solved, will free up some much-needed time for character issues. We must increase our commitment to character education, all the while continuing the important task of firearm education. The hunter education manual has thirty-six pages on firearm equipment and safety and another ten pages on muzzleloaders. This accounts for about one-half of the pages in the manual, excluding the review chapter. Roughly the same proportion of time is spent in class on this topic. That is, about one-half of the nine-hour class is about firearms. The manual, by contrast, covers ethics in six pages and wildlife conservation in seven pages, and hunting skills in ten pages. In this often-cursory treatment, students are supposed to learn ethics and responsibility, conservation, wildlife management, habitat management, carrying capacity, and wildlife identification as well as hunting skills.

To suggest a reduced role for firearm education will be perceived as heresy. But we could divide the task into two. First, book-learning about firearms and their workings could become a part of the newly emerging online hunter-education course. This would require students to know about shotgun shells, rifles, and the various parts of these firearms. They could even be tested on these questions before they actually attend the hunter education class. A second part of this is the practical training in firing a gun and field safety in its use. This hands-on aspect is already present in hunter education courses, and by reducing the in-class time devoted to memory materials, this component could even be expanded.

I think it is important to remind ourselves that firearms are but one means by which we might acquire animals. Hunting embraces many other means including the technology of fishing and trapping. Yet, unfortunately, firearms have come to be the symbol of hunting. It is time for hunter-education courses and hunting organizations to change this perception. We must endeavor to break the link between hunting and firearm ownership issues. This connection, so carefully forged and strengthened by firearms advocates and the firearm industry, would have the public believe that the right to hunt and the right to own a firearm are synonymous. They are not. Firearms are one tool for acquiring animals, but hunting has existed and can exist without this tool. Firearms advocates are riding piggyback on the general public acceptance of hunting, but this extra weight may eventually lay hunting flat.

Underlying all divisions in hunting by kind of implement used, whether by spears or shotgun, fly rods or harpoons, are the skills necessary for hunting. These skills come down to finding animals, getting close enough to acquire them, and then having the skill to actually make the capture or kill. One skill that is mentioned in *Today's Hunter* is game calling. This skill has genuine "split rail" appeal and offers the opportunity for a deep exploration of animal behavior. It is a way to get close to wildlife, whether one chooses to hunt or not. Another skill in this same elemental category is fly-tying, which invites one to explore the food chains and ecology of fish. Once one gets close enough to wildlife, the various tools available become important, and the use of these tools in some cases requires great skill also. But it is a mistake to concentrate too much on skillful use of one tool, firearms, at the expense of the other more elemental skills. *Today's Hunter* asserts correctly that hunters should "know their quarry" because it will "increase your success and add to the enjoyment of the experience as well."[7] But surely we need to supplement this knowledge with real practice in the skills of reading natural signs and stealthy approach to wildlife. These elemental skills are closely connected to environmental virtues.

Conservation, Ecology, and Wildlife

Chapter Nine, the last chapter in *Today's Hunter,* is "Wildlife Conservation." It covers lessons in wildlife management, habitat conservation, carrying capacity, as well as the principles of wildlife management and conservation and wildlife identification. That is a lot in a few pages. In line with this, the overall message seems to be that sportsmen should let the expert wildlife managers do their job and manage the resource. Now, it may be that the authors of this manual realize that their audience is young people just getting their hunting licenses, and so need to concentrate on that, but I think we must do more. We must start these young people on a path of conservation, husbandry, and civic activism. These are the socially recognized marks of the environmental virtues inculcated by field sports. To truncate the education of sportsmen by allowing them to relinquish their historical role in wildlife conservation is to undermine the sportsman thesis. The hunter's manual makes it appear that everything is under control, but every sportsman knows this is not true. There are constant environmental challenges to hunting and fishing: maintaining roadless areas, restoring habitat for cold-water fish, and so on. It is just unconscionable to reduce the role of sportsmen to filling out questionnaires and buying hunting licenses to support management as suggested in the manual.

With regard to conservation and wildlife, the role of the sportsman as activist is muted by those very institutions assigned to the task of protecting game and wildlife. Each state has its departments of environmental conservation and the United States Fish and Wildlife Service develops national policies. These institutions have slowly and unwittingly eroded an active conservation role for sportsmen. It is commonplace now for field sports to be described by official state publications as "an effective wildlife management tool."[8] This becomes a defense of hunting and angling when they are challenged: we are only trying to help everybody by keeping the numbers of deer, moose, geese, etc. in check. It sounds good to most people. There is even a kind of scientific detachment to it when it is pointed out that season length and bag limits are determined by population surveys, and that "X" number of animals need to be taken in order to keep the populations within the "carrying capacity" of the land.

There are, however, some serious problems with this educational philosophy.

First, while some game species are indeed liable to outgrow the carrying capacity of the land, many will not. It would be ridiculous to say that we keep grouse, trout, and many other small game populations from growing too large by our activities, although perhaps rabbits might fit the game management model.

Second, and more importantly, to see field sports as "tools" is to ignore and even derail the sportsman thesis: that they develop environmental character. Field sports are capable of developing virtue because they are practices *for their own sake.* They are leisure activities and have excellence as their goal. This search for excellence is made more attractive by the accompanying pleasure one receives in making progress. The environmental virtues of field sports are a consequence of this search for excellence. When the activity is not done for its own sake but for the sake of some utilitarian end, such as a "tool for wildlife management," it is deflected from this path, at least as far as the public perception of the activities is concerned. While sportsmen who still practice field sports for their own sake may disagree, their public image is compromised.

The chance to guide environmental awareness and biotic perception is valuable. In the hunter education course we should take this opportunity to make connections between the characteristics of animals and their evolution and ecological relations. This educational strategy will require more time be devoted to this section of the course. It might include actual practice in reading natural signs of tracks, scat, and sounds and linking them to the biotic community that supports the animals involved. Conscientious and responsible butchering of animals offers another great opportunity to learn about ecological connections. It is important to remember that we needn't be experts in ecology to teach these connections; our goal is to plant the seeds of biotic perception and environmental awareness. These are the intellectual virtues one attains by gaining knowledge of the ecology and evolution of the species one hunts or fishes. It is an expansive curiosity about the natural world. This is surely not thwarted by hunter education as it is presented. But what is blocked is the natural evolution of this awareness in the direction of husbandry and activism.

Conclusion

Sportsman education needs to move in several new directions. Realizing that good habits are only established by long-term commitment, courses must make practice central. This will require devoting less time to firearm knowledge in class and more time to hunting skills. Environmental awareness and biotic perception must grow from knowledge about wildlife and habitat. As we shall see in the next chapter, our conception of game and the role of sportsmen in game management will need to be altered.

Chapter Thirteen: Attitudes about Game and Wildlife

Hunting and fishing are arts of acquisition. The material goods acquired are derived from the bodies of animals: birds, mammals, fish, and others. In addition to these material goods, participants in field sports seek the good of acquiring environmental virtue. Coinciding with the evolution of the sportsman thesis, from Plato to the present, are debates between sportsmen and others about the class of animals considered as suitable quarry for sportsmen, called "game" animals. Not all wild animals are selected for this status. For Plato, the premier quarry was probably rabbits that could be chased by men on horseback. The hierarchy of game animals has shifted according to availability and convention. Once, the noble hart was the only animal worthy of royal attention.[1] Now, some say the Atlantic salmon is the "king of the game fish." Other animals are relegated to the status of "trash fish" or "varmints" by hunters and anglers. But what should we make of such judgments by sportsmen?

The issues surrounding game policies are extremely complex both legally and scientifically. Sportsmen seek to influence these policies by sometimes calling for reduced limits and shortened seasons and at other times for expanded opportunities to hunt and fish. They thus seek to influence policy decisions about stocking and season length. They may suggest and actively participate in habitat improvements. These suggestions are sometimes met with opposition from within the community of sportsmen, professionals in wildlife areas, and others interested in wildlife issues. My interest in this chapter is finding a way to frame some of these debates such that questions about environmental virtues are central. In particular, I've argued that if field sports are to retain their capacity to generate virtue, they must be guided by the quest for excellence, a full aesthetic experience connecting them to the land, and an ongoing curiosity about their biotic community. These goals must also come to guide debates about game animals as well.

Definitions of Game

Definitions of "game animals" have always been contested, reflecting changing perceptions of wildlife. Aristocratic ideas of social status and hierarchy have frequently been imposed by use of the concept of game. I've discussed the historical connection between nineteenth-century sportsmen and the reestablishment of wildlife populations.[2] The term "game" as used in this country found its traditional meaning in the policies and laws developed by those gentlemen-sportsmen. These originators of the North American sportsman thesis, like their European cousins, conceptually set aside those animals they thought worthy of being hunted by people such as themselves. In contrast, some hunters and fishermen took any usable animal.[3] From the vast number of wild animals that could be eaten or used in other ways, some are selected as game.

The term "game" as applied to animals has a wide and deep history. The various *Oxford English Dictionary* entries for it run to over four pages of that tiny print only found in the *OED*. Game animals, as "wild animals or birds such as are pursued, caught or killed in the chase" is a usage that goes back at least to the early fourteenth century. In some cases, game animals were only those one could hunt using trained dogs. An 1862 British act proclaims game to include hares, pheasants, partridges, etc. Another definition of "game" that seems relevant to this discussion is that of a "game fowl," which is a bird with fighting spirit, pluck, and endurance. Game fish are also mentioned in this sense. Finally, game may refer to the flesh of game animals.

How, in light of the fact that game animals have always had something to do with changing social status and group membership, do we define "game animals" today? We could, to beg the question, just list all those species identified by states and nations as game. This would be a very long list even if game fish are not included. There are surely some inconsistencies in this list as one moves from state to state or nation to nation. For example, in Texas doves are legal game animals, but they are not in New York. Sportsmen will always consider trout to be a game fish but probably not carp. The list of game animals is historically evolving, and there's every reason to expect it to be different at different times and cultural location. The factors that account for these changes are many but include availability, management priorities, traditions, and desires of hunters and anglers. These factors and others are reflected in the various state and federal codes concerning fish and game. It is a very complicated business: the State of California Code for fish and game runs to 16,541 sections. Regardless of our rigor in developing this list, it would not answer the question of what we *should* mean by "game," only what we as a matter of fact do mean at this point.

Several efforts to define game animals are instructive. Gasset, in his *Meditations on Hunting,* proposes that game animals are those "creatures with regard to which the only adequate behavior is to hunt them" because he thinks humans have a "predatory intention," which is excited by the presence of game animals.[4] But if some animals have the power to excite the predatory intention in us, that power remains mysterious and many will counter that they go happily through their days with no awareness of any urge to chase and acquire every rabbit or duck they happen to see.

The anthropologist Heidi Dahles, by contrast, actually surveys hunters about what they value in "game" animals. They, she concludes,

> . . . *elaborate on the behavior and characteristics of the animals they are chasing. What they usually appreciate them for is strength, beauty, perfection of fur or feather, keen perception and intelligence, a massive trophy, quick and unpredictable movements, cleverness, alertness and courage. . . . The common denominator of these features is a fighting spirit.*[5]

The characteristics listed are attributed to certain kinds of animals. If animals are valued for their "fighting spirit" this is because, again according to Dahles, such animals "play the game according to the hunter's rules."[6] Dahles further asserts that this set of characteristics has mostly replaced for hunters the edibility of game as the motive for pursuing these animals.

Definitions of "game animal," then, seem to range between a "real" definition of the sort offered by Ortega, where there is some real characteristic of certain animal species that sets them off as game, and a more socially constructed view wherein animal species are selected out by traits humans impose upon them. However this debate is resolved, hunters and anglers are not shy about making pronouncements about the relative status of certain animals. It is these judgments we need to evaluate in terms of environmental virtues.

Game and Character

Debates about game animals between sportsmen typically concern three things. First, there are debates about the relative number of game animals: too few or too many. Too few salmon are in the river or too many deer are ruining their habitat. These opinions about *quantity* are mixed with attitudes about the relative *quality* of certain species: carp are bottom-feeding trash-fish some say, others reply that carp are great game fish; walleyes don't fight but rainbow trout do, etc. These debates are complicated also when game population size is thought to be significantly affected by other kinds of wildlife. So, for instance, double-crested cormorants are despised by some, both because they are thought to eat and thus reduce the numbers of salmon and trout available to be caught and because they are not particularly beautiful—there is little qualitatively to recommend them. By contrast loons, whose fish-eating habits mirror those of cormorants, are depicted on posters and made into cuddly stuffed toys. Third, in addition to debates concerning quantity and quality, there are those based upon the origins of the species: are they native or imported, stocked or wild? Again, these attitudes are often mixed within issues of stocking or restoring species of animals.

Recognizing that many of these opinions are based on anecdote, hearsay, and personal experience, it is incumbent upon sportsmen to guide their debates and actions with a well-honed practical reason. Opinions will always differ on some of these topics, but what is crucial is that when actual practices are contemplated for action, they be guided by the environmental virtues. Since sportsmen acquire animals both for the material good and the good of character development, we might explore what a person with such reason would say about these issues. In the past, animals were sometimes selected for general character traits. Hunting dangerous animals might develop courage; sly ones stealth; fast ones fleetness. But once we set our sights on environmental virtues, these characteristics are no longer germane. We must instead evaluate debates about game in terms of the virtues of an ecological conscience, environmental awareness, and aesthetic competence. We must keep in mind that the sportsman thesis is a hypothesis about education and so policies must make allowances for various ages and abilities. This is especially important when these attitudes are used to support practices and policies with widespread effects.[7]

Biotic perception is practical reason in the environmental sphere. This holistic ability to do the right thing at the right time will be employed by sportsmen on a case-by-case basis. We can't expect general prescriptions and abstract ethical principles to guide us. The salient features of each case will differ. However, establishing some rules of thumb will help.

One implication of the intellectual virtue of environmental awareness is that sportsmen need to know as much as possible about the ecology of the animals they pursue before any policies are endorsed. This knowledge must align the best science available with a nascent awareness of ecological knowledge. Our judgments about population sizes and policies related to this should be based on evidence and not anecdote.

Second, the behavior and physical characteristics of game species are also important. Sportsmen sometimes assert that some game species are beautiful and others ugly. But these judgments must be evaluated in terms of biotic perception and not in their usual meaning. The beauty of the behavior and physical characteristics of animals are results of their evolution. For example, the beauty of brook trout or grouse should reside not simply in how they "look" to humans but in our appreciation of the way those characteristics are causal consequences of their long evolution as species. Their coloration and camouflage, speed and caution, are properties they have as a result of their relationships with human and nonhuman predators, members of their own species, and a multitude of other evolutionary factors. Because some have been prey species for humans, these characteristics have come to be admired. Indeed, some species have evolved expressly because of their interactions with humans: not just domesticated animals but wild ones as well. Bears, mountain lions, and some spring creek brown trout clearly alter their behavior as a result of their contact with humans. Because these animals have evolved in this way, they require the highest levels of skillfulness and awareness on the part of the sportsman. This beauty is not just a kind of prettiness. Brook trout in spawning colors are really pretty. But bowfins (according to some, an ugly fish) are also beautiful in the evolutionary sense described.

Third, when we judge that game animals should be *wild* in origin, we mean they are indicators and natural signs of the biotic health of the ecosystems in which they reside.[8] They are wild because they are *from* the wild; they say by their presence that the covert or stream in which they reside is a healthy one.[9] The wildness of game is not determined by their behavior but by their biotic community.

Leopold sums this all up by saying that certain species, such as the ruffed grouse, have a "motive power," which enlivens the autumn woods.

> *Everybody knows, for example, that the autumn landscape in the north woods is the land, plus a red maple, plus a ruffed grouse. In terms of conventional physics, the grouse represents only a millionth of either the mass or the energy of an acre. Yet subtract the grouse and the whole thing is dead. An enormous amount of some kind of motive power has been lost.*[10]

The enormous "motive power" supplied by the grouse is determined by the gauge of biotic perception. Part of what is meant is that game species like grouse are natural signs of the health and diversity of their biotic communities. Grouse play this role, as do brook trout, salmon, and turkeys. It is also true that we tend to focus on certain qualities of game animals. We appreciate aesthetic features of coloration, size, and strength. But our reason for appreciating these properties should have more to do with the evolutionary history of those animals than our conventional imposition of standards.

Certain species of animals are popular game animals because they have this power. White-tail deer, for instance, are exceptionally wary when they are hunted, provide an excellent source of meat, and are natural signs of the health of the biotic community in which they reside. This last claim is, of course, subject to the qualification in that they are quite capable of extending their range to other, less-welcome biotic communities. When pheasants are stocked in geographical areas not suited to their survival, they are certainly still good to eat and have spectacular aesthetic characteristics, but they say little as natural signs.

That they need to be restocked at all should be a clue as to their suitability as game for that region.

Given the revised sportsman thesis, the compass point for game animals should be that they are wild in that they are members of the biotic community in which sportsmen enter. They are parts of the traditional food chains in which humans are a part. The degree to which the concept of game is deflected from this point should provoke our ecological conscience to change course. Species that are thus wild food are game in the primary sense.

In order to better explain and illustrate this I will consider two debates, the first about game and wildness and the second about the connection between game and food.

The Value of Stocked Game

Are wild game animals more valuable than stocked? What attitude should sportsmen have about stocking programs? Leopold believes that the "recreational value of a head of game is inverse to the artificiality of its origin, and hence in a broad way to the intensity of the system of game management which produces it."[11] What Leopold is getting at is the preference hunters and anglers should have for "wild" game. Thus he says a native trout taken from a high Rocky Mountain stream has more value that a hatchery-raised brown trout caught in a polluted stream in the East. The hatchery trout, stocked for pond or stream fishing, has a lower aesthetic value because their wildness and beauty are muted by their artificial origins. Because of their power to alter these values of game, management policies are of central concern to sportsmen. State and federal stocking agencies are subject to many pressures. The public demand for more game animals must be tempered by the value of game for not only food but also skills required, beauty, and biotic significance.

By contrast, non-stocked game animals, such as the grouse, are one true measure of the health of an ecological community. The aesthetic properties of the grouse are produced by the ecological community in which it resides. The grouse is beautifully adopted for survival, given that everything is in ecological order. It eats almost anything: berries, insects, buds. It can walk on the snow and burrow underneath it. Its camouflage is superb. It is fast in flight and acrobatic on the wing. These properties, which test the skills of grouse hunters, are results of the evolution of the species. So the beauty of grouse is not derived solely from their interesting, indeed fascinating, ways of surviving, but also from the way these properties signify the health of the biotic community to which the grouse belongs. A game animal like the grouse represents significance beyond its physical characteristics and behavior.

It is crucial for hunters and anglers to be aware of the differences between stocked and wild game. To the degree that we acquiesce to the pursuit of stocked game we relinquish to others our need to know the wild biotic community and the conscience that requires we care about its continuation. This awareness and the conscience to act are sorely lacking in many cases. Cold-water lakes suitable for salmon and lake trout are allowed, with little concern, to become warm-water fisheries for bass and pike. Critical woodcock habitat becomes old-growth forest, and there is no comment.

Game animals are stocked to increase or maintain their numbers. For example, Atlantic salmon are stocked in places they once flourished in the attempt to reestablish them. Turkeys were reintroduced for the same reason, but they seem to flourish now and there is no reason to keep stocking them. Besides stocking there are other factors that influence the health of game populations. One is predator policy, i.e., the acknowledgement of the relation between game animal populations and the species of animals that prey upon them. While it was once thought that fewer predators meant more game, this has been found to be a mistake in many cases. Another factor influencing game populations is attitudes about hunting and fishing. Some suburbs have extended into wild areas and have experienced problems with deer, bears, and mountain lions as a result.[12] As these areas become unplanned sanctuaries for prey animals, they tend to attract predators as well.

Sportsmen must keep several things in mind when we think about these issues. First, the number of animals we acquire is not important. This is an artificial measure of excellence. Second, the health of the biotic community is paramount and stocking must be measured against this standard. Third, credible scientific evidence must inform our decisions about policies regarding predators. There has always been too much prejudice and anecdotal evidence used in making decisions about predators. Biotic holism, if it is to mean anything, must move us to see the connections between our environmental actions and subsequent problems. For instance, stocking large numbers of fish has increased predation of those fish by birds and parasites. Intellectual hubris is a vice here as elsewhere.

So sportsmen should be cautious in recommending or accepting game stocking. Such programs should be required to show that they are parts of broader endeavors to improve biotic health in general and not mask signs of disease by artificial means.

Varmints, Predators, and Trash Fish

There are several incidents from my childhood experiences with hunting and fishing that are relevant here. I used to get to go pheasant hunting with my relatives. They insisted I carry a stick as if it was a shotgun, and I would walk along with them through the (very) tall cornfields. One day, as we came out of the field, my grandfather saw a hawk sitting on a fence post, and he immediately shot it. I wasn't really surprised by this because I had been taught that hawks and owls eat pheasants and reduce their numbers. Of course, such an attitude and such behavior now shock me. Similarly, we used to fish a lake that was (so we believed) over-populated with perch, and as we caught them instead of the sought-after crappies or walleyes, we would bang them against the side of the boat to kill them and then throw them back in the water.

What are we to make of this clearly unsavory bias? It continues today with the shooting of prairie dogs and bow-hunting for carp. This is a complicated issue because there are numerous factors at work. First, there are state and federal policies that actually encourage the reduction in numbers of certain species. There are lakes so crowded with northern pike that special regulations allow one to keep as many as one wants of any size. There, pike are considered "trash fish," as also in parts of California, where they were illegally introduced and then the attempt was made to remove them from the lakes where they were placed. Besides policy, there are general hunter and angler perceptions and misperceptions of beauty. As mentioned, double-crested cormorants provide an interesting example. They are, by and large, despised by salmon and trout anglers because they seem to prey on these fish after they are stocked. But I think there is also something about their look that bothers anglers and even justifies their reduction to them. A third factor, besides policies and perceptions, is property damage or the fear of such. This motivates some ranchers to advocate for the shooting of prairie dogs, coyotes, and wolves and some farmers to think that since foxes are eating their chickens (if, that is, the chickens get out in the yard anymore!) they should be controlled. That is, some wild animals are seen as competitors with domesticated plants and animals and are therefore reduced to increase the value of farm-raised products.

These factors make it very difficult to provide a neat, ethical decision about policies of hunting and fishing for animals we don't intend to eat. Calling them "varmints" or "trash fish" just muddies the waters. The more biologically inclined might be moved to begin talking of "competitive predators" rather than varmints and trash fish. This is something of an advance because predators of game and domesticated animals are fairly clearly identifiable. While there are certainly great advances in the science of this, we might look again at Leopold's classic analysis of this issue in *Game Management*. Leopold's main thesis in the chapter called "Predator Control" is that the policies and practices at that time were based in large part on unsupported assumptions and hasty generalizations. He advocates a more scientific and quantitative approach based on field studies and accurate historical data. Of particular relevance is Leopold's admonition to hunters that they often act out of ignorance and self-interest. They would do well to study the actual role of predators with regard to game management. The terms "varmint," "vermin," "trash fish," and so on are often reflections of unwarranted hunter and angler impressions.

This leaves open the question of whether some animals may be hunted by sportsmen because they are not food but rather competitive predators. I believe that the answer to this question must be "no," except in the most extreme circumstances. My reasons for this are based on the increasingly convincing scientific evidence that predators have a valuable role to play in ecosystems as well as the principle of caution, which states that just because we don't know what some species are good for, doesn't mean we are allowed to eliminate them. As Leopold said, we shouldn't throw things away simply because we don't see their importance at this point in time.[13] In addition, activities like shooting prairie dogs severely restrict the scope of hunting, leaving out the good derived from the body of the animal. However, this is a debate that enlivens the revised sportsman thesis, and its initiation reflects that of discovering what truly is the biotic good.

One related consideration is the extent to which hunting or fishing for non-food species is relinquishing the central goals required by the sportsman thesis. After all, a justification for participating in predator-control hunts is often that doing so enacts some needed reduction in that population in the name of game management. Here the goal of the activity is determined by state and federal agencies, and the hunting becomes a means for the achievement of this goal. As I've argued, motives for hunting and angling are subject to change and slide between excellence and more utilitarian purposes, but sportsmen should at the minimum be on the alert for the pressure of institutions to modify them. Consuming the body of an animal is such a powerful connection to the biotic community that it should not be relinquished without careful thought.

Conclusion

Classifying game animals expands and contracts, given the swings in opinion as to their definition. I am urging that for the environmental sportsman, debates about the numbers, qualities, and origins of these species be decided by asking whether these species are wild food. This implies in particular a critical attitude about stocking and an attempt to go beyond the use of derogatory categories as justification for hunting for or not fishing for certain species. Calling a species a varmint or vermin does not justify actions in the absence of other compelling reasons.

Chapter Fourteen: Conflicting Visions of Outdoor Recreation

Increasingly, field sports find themselves competing with other forms of outdoor recreation. Should streams be devoted to fishing or kayaking or both? Should wildlife management areas be open for both hunting and birding? Should motor enthusiasts be allowed to access hunting areas on all-terrain vehicles?[1] The resolution of these ongoing will require more attention than I can devote in this chapter. What I will do is frame them in terms of environmental virtues, as I did with those more internal debates addressed in the last chapter. There is a political reason for this: for field sports to survive, and even flourish, they must make common cause with suitable alternative forms of outdoor recreation. When hunting and angling were seen as *the* kinds of outdoor recreation that develop gentlemen and their noble virtues, this was not much of an issue. But now, because of competition from so many other kinds of outdoor recreation, sportsmen need to form alliances to conserve both wild and cultivated areas suitable for these activities. The question is how other forms of outdoor recreation are to be directed toward environmental virtues? What are the basic requirements of outdoor recreation that allow for and enable this expansion? Finally, how are debates between different forms of recreation to be framed?

Outdoor Recreation without Handrails

In *Mountains Without Handrails*, Joseph Sax makes a persuasive case for the preservation of national parks and similar areas because they stimulate and maintain "reflective or contemplative recreation." Sax writes against the background of what he sees as the increasing degradation of national parks by supplying "handrails," or means of making the experience safer and more convenient, especially for motorized tourism. He cites field sports along with mountaineering as models for the kinds of recreation he promotes.[2]

. The fundamental purpose of reflective or contemplative recreation, as Sax sees it, is as an experimental test of an ethical proposition. Such recreation tests the "will to dominate and the inclination to submissiveness" and repays their transcendence with profound gratification.[3]

Reflective or contemplative recreation are those activities that confront one with ethical choices that must be worked through. This is like the difficulty of maintaining one's balance on a slippery summit trail, with the dangerous dropoffs of domination on one side and submission on the other. Sax further explains the nature of the recreation he recommends in these terms:

> *Neither the setting nor the activity in itself seems to be decisive; rather it is the presence of something capable of engaging, rather than merely occupying the individual—a stimulus for intensity of experience, for the full involvement of the senses and the mind.*[4]

But what is this "something" that engages and stimulates the senses and the mind? It emerges from the interaction between settings and activities, between places and doings. It is this stimulus that accounts for the intense interest shown by some anglers, hunters, and mountain climbers. The existence of this "something" means that we cannot simply discuss "outdoor activities" without constant reference to the attitudes and goals of the participants. We cannot condemn or praise certain activities as a whole based upon an ideal or customary image of them. Outdoor activities, like field sports, take place in certain kinds of setting in which "attitude" is crucial. Having an environmental character is one way we've referred to this attitude. This includes appreciation of the intensity of the sensory experience to which the biotic community contributes.

The sportsman thesis has been developed by reference to field sports, but there are clearly other outdoor activities that may be pursued in conjunction with field sports or independently of them that may lead to similar ethical challenges and intense rewards. Sportsmen must open avenues of cooperation with these related "no handrail" outdoor recreations because their common natural settings are the ground out of which grows environmental virtues. The virtues arising from different outdoor activities, while not precisely the same as those developed by field sports, are nevertheless, virtues in the right direction. These other outdoor recreations also are capable of moving their practitioners in the direction of the land ethic.

The Varieties of Outdoor Recreation

I will not define outdoor recreation, but some examples of it will keep us focused in the right areas. Besides field sports, activities as diverse as birding, rock climbing, and four-wheeling are considered to be members of this group. Recognizing which activities are closely aligned with field sports is an important first step in their comparative evaluation; we then begin to move the issue away from simply "what I want to do." That is, it might initially seem that one's choice as to which outdoor recreation to pursue is immune from criticism, as if all outdoor recreation is created equal. If someone decides to go four-wheeling, rock climbing, or fly fishing, that is up to that person and there's no question of why. In fact, the person might well be offended should one have the temerity to question his or her choice. Part of this attitude results from our rather peculiar views regarding recreation in general. There seems to be no need for justification here, whereas if it is a job that someone is taking, then we have all sorts of questions: how much money, what are the benefits, how many hours per week, etc. Taking a job is a decision open to critical review whereas deciding to rock climb is not. Even raising the issue will likely warrant a resentful stare instead of an answer.

In order to provide a way to begin to raise questions about outdoor activities, let us look at some that are closely related to field sports. First, field sports are activities or arts of acquisition. There are some other activities that count as arts of acquisition as well. These include mushroom collecting, wild-plant collecting, and insect collecting. Second, there are training activities for using animals in outdoor activities, like training hunting dogs or horses. Included is the venerable art of falconry, where raptors are trained to hunt. These activities may be integrated into field sports or other acquisitive activities but in some instances become ends in themselves. (I've recently read about training dogs to find truffles!) Third, there are arts of observation such as birding, wildlife photography, sketching, and the challenging activities of tracking animals and making inferences from scat and other natural signs. As in the case of training activities, these are now often pursued as ends in themselves even though they are still integral skills in hunting and fishing. Fourth, there are husbandry activities of nature restoration and game farming. These activities attempt to restore the biotic health of a degraded community and are related to gardening and other agricultural pursuits. Sometimes these activities involve the restoration of wildlife, sometimes the removal of invasive species. It seems clear that these four kinds of outdoor activities are capable of integration with field sports and indeed often accompany them. This is, of course, because they are all offspring of hunting and gathering, the most elemental outdoor activities of all.

Activities of practical reason attempt to achieve some goal, whether it is a product, performance, or the acquisition of an animal. There are other goals as well. The achievement of these goals are more or less under the influence of factors beyond the control of the participant—call it chance, luck, or fate. At one end of this continuum are those activities where one has almost total control over the outcome, building models for example. At the other end are activities where there is some control, but so many other factors are involved that I previously called them "stochastic." Natural processes and events, such as weather, wind, and tide, are constant companions for these activities. The reading of these signs becomes a necessity.

Activities whose goals are such that their achievement depends on natural factors are best able to inculcate environmental virtues. This is perhaps what Sax is getting at when he references that "something" that engages the mind and senses of participants. These factors become salient to practical reasoning insofar as they attune participants to causal connections and their maintenance. Arts such as mushrooming, dog training, and restoration projects are equally nature-salient, and as such capable of enabling environmental virtues. Gardening and wildlife photography are too. While these virtues are not identically realized in each of the other activities, from the point of view of sportsmen, those who participate in them should be friends and allies.

Yet when one asks outdoorsy students to list their favorite activities, the former kinds are rarely picked. Rather, they chose endurance and thrill activities like mountaineering, rock climbing, white-water kayaking, backcountry skiing, and surfing. With some exceptions, chance natural factors are important to these activities, i.e., to do the activity requires the rock, whitewater, backcountry, and surf. But the ecological connections of food chains are mostly absent. The natural signs are limited to those few salient to making it up the cliff or through the white water. Of course, these adventure activities have greater access to and awareness of natural signs than motorized versions. In activities such as ATV riding or snowmobiling, the location seems only the means to ride the machine.

Activities cannot be evaluated without frequent reference to the attitudes and goals of participants. After all, if we as sportsmen justifiably complain about the stereotyping of our activities, we must be sensitive to the same charge levied at us in looking at other activities. As Sax points out, the quality of the experience one has in an outdoor activity is influenced by two external factors: First, there is the setting for the activity: mountains, lakes, beaches, oceans, marshes, etc. Second, the activity itself calls for certain tools, skills, and restraints. Fly fishing requires the use of fly rods and flies and the skills necessary to use them; for water skiing, a boat, a rope, and necessary skills are also required. Some activities also invite us to ever-higher levels of expertise and present us with challenges to our ethics as well as to our skills. With these, a third factor is crucial: the relative importance of reading natural signs. It is through this stimulus that we make connections to the biotic good, which is all-important for developing environmental virtues.

This raises several important questions about the quality of the experience in doing the activity and therefore the power of the activity to move us in the direction of the land ethic. Since the setting for activities like field sports is a healthy and diverse biotic community, we might ask about the centrality of this for other activities. Clearly, if one wants to fish for brook trout, there is an expansive set of biotic requirements concerning water quality, temperature, structure, insect life, etc. Awareness of these connections and requirements is exercised and rewarded by this activity. So one important question we might ask is the extent to which the activity demands the development of environmental awareness? To what extent is one's environmental awareness engaged and drawn outward? Second, since outdoor activities should be aimed at the development of excellence (or else why are we doing them?), we might reasonably ask whether they demand a persistent and pervasive commitment by participants to high standards as set by respected members of the community? Finally, is the aesthetic experience not only intense, as suggested by Sax, but also dependent upon the ability to correctly interpret the natural signs salient to the activity? These sorts of questions can be used to begin an evaluation of outdoor activities.

Cases

If we need to know the extent to which the quality of the experience of the participants in an activity depends on there being a healthy and diverse biotic community, then we must consider a range of cases. At one extreme, and again depending on the intentions of the participants, we might place various speed/thrill activities such as mountain-bike racing or downhill-ski racing. The participants in these activities literally fly right over the terrain; there's little awareness at all of the biotic community. Activities performed in this way don't teach one to read the signs of health or illness of a biotic community or require one to read the language of ecological natural signs.

Consider birding by contrast. This activity might require a sophisticated understanding of natural signs: bird songs, flashes of color, flight patterns and profiles, vegetation, etc. Birding is an environmental portal to other areas of natural-sign reading. To be an expert birder is to have these skills and more. But birding isn't just watching the birds that happen to be around; there is an ecological conscience that develops regarding the habitats and flyways of birds. There is an active concern for the well-being of bird species and the habitats that allow them to flourish. Birding is also a consuming experience, deeply meaningful. It builds communities with likeminded birders; a civic sense develops.

Between these there are other cases. Many college-aged students love the thrill of rock climbing. Can we find ways to encourage the development of environmental virtues here? Certainly there is already a basis for ethical restraint in the movement to leave no trace and avoid certain techniques that might do damage. There is also a prescription against climbing too close to nesting birds. Teachers of climbing skills would do well to expand upon these restraints by encouraging participants to expand their environmental awareness to the life cycles of raptors and the vegetation one might expect to discover in these areas. An ecological conscience might also be encouraged in the care for the continuation of the biotic community in which one climbs.

Canoeing is another widely popular outdoor activity. Some boats are frequently transported from one body of water to another. This raises the problem of the transport of unwanted invasive plants and animals from one place to another. As a result, some states have made it a priority to inform boaters about this danger and supply them with information about the need to clean their boats and other items before they are transferred. This is another way of expanding environmental virtues to this outdoor recreation.

All of this is pretty standard stuff. But these cases give us the means to critically examine some of the more offensive forms of outdoor recreation. Zooming around a desert landscape on an all-terrain vehicle will clearly be low on any scale of activities judged by the virtues they inculcate, regardless of the intentions of the participants.

Resolving Conflicts

Is there a way to ethically decide which outdoor activities should be given precedence in cases of conflict? For instance, when anglers find themselves pitted against kayakers over the issue of water-flow levels in dammed rivers: anglers want to have water levels roughly constant to benefit the invertebrates and thus the trout, but kayakers want pulsed releases to increase the thrill of the ride. Who ought to get precedence? Hunters sometimes find themselves in conflict with hikers and other trail users who don't want to be around firearms. To resolve some of these cases rationally, one needs to develop a general view about the value of outdoor activities and especially their relations to environmental concerns. The usual approach seems to be unfortunately loaded toward economic calculation: the decisions follow the money. Thus, if there is more money to be made in allowing snowmobiles into Yellowstone than not, then that is what seems to happen. This, as Leopold pointed out, is lopsided and ultimately ruinous both for recreation and for the biotic communities involved. Another popular but dangerous decision-making procedure is taking polls. While in many cases citizens reach excellent decisions there are egregious exceptions. We are thus led back to consider whether there might be an ethically justifiable way of making such decisions.

I suggest we use the questions about environmental virtues as a framework for making these tough choices. It seems fair to at least ask motorized sports enthusiasts to relate their activity to environmental concern, or increased awareness of natural processes. Field sports will do well in answering these questions if the participants have accepted the ultimate requirements of these activities.

Conclusion

Outdoor activities other than field sports should be encouraged to emulate the model of the sportsman thesis. These activities are already the stimulus for the intense experiences identified by Sax. They are open to influence by making connections between them and the environmental awareness of the biotic communities in which they are practiced. Also, an enhanced ecological conscience is possible by emphasizing the fragility of the lands upon which and in which these activities take place. In some cases, such as off-road vehicle use and other motorized activities, these connections will be stretched to the breaking point, and so these activities must be judged deficient on environmental grounds.

Chapter Fifteen: The Sportsman Myth

I began this work expressing some skepticism about the plausibility of the sportsman thesis, that grand old belief that field sports generate virtue. How can activities generate virtue? Which virtues are generated? Since it seems only some people are successfully inoculated by virtue, how are the failures explained? What I've discovered is that field sports are *capable* of generating virtue because they are activities of practical reason, where skill and mastery play pivotal roles. And field sports are activities *capable* of being chosen for excellence: participants might be motivated by good mentors and self-regard to participate in field sports as leisure activities in the classical sense. The extent to which virtue is generated depends crucially on these factors.

I have argued that the virtues field-sport educators should aim to develop are environmental, defined in terms of the biotic good. Only if this good is preeminent will the virtues of an ecological conscience, environmental awareness, and aesthetic competence be capable of withstanding serious objections to field sports. A paragon of environmental perception, with these virtues smoothly articulated, provides a model for the rest of us who continually struggle with the nagging tugs of vice. Sportsmen live up to this ideal more or less, but they are at least motivated by the quest for it. The sportsman thesis then, once it is revised in these ways, becomes again an idea whose prominence will reconnect sportsmanship and conservation.

Ted Kerasote, a defender of field sports, describes what he calls the "exhausted myth" of the conservationist sportsman. Part of this myth has it that sportsmen "know nature and wildlife best." But, he points out, hunters and anglers don't always support policies designed to conserve wildlife habitat. The myth has it that hunters are disciplined and reluctant takers-of-life, but stories in the news of irresponsible shooting and fishing have it otherwise. The myth has it that sportsmen are virtuous and courageous, but again the evidence is weak. Finally, if sportsmen value simplicity and an "honest interaction with nature," why do they need all the gadgets?[1] Kerasote believes that with great effort field sports can be reformed, and furthermore thinks they are worth it. With this I certainly agree. And while he doesn't discuss the philosophical bases for this reform, I think we can now see that this vision of the sportsman is not a myth but rather an ideal.

It is an ideal in that it sets before us a possible achievement. When we begin this journey as youths, this goal is far distant. We make incremental progress under the guidance of others and our own commitment to excellence. My task has not been to make this path easier but to make its route clear and compelling. If field sports are to retain their ethical basis, they must promote this ideal of excellence, virtue, and the biotic good.

BIBLIOGRAPHY

Adams, Carol J. 1994. *Neither Man Nor Beast.* New York: Continuum.

Ambrose, Stephen E. 1996. *Undaunted Courage.* New York: Touchstone.

Annas, Julia. 1995. "Virtue as a Skill." *International Journal of Philosophical Studies* 3 (2): 227-243.

Argyros, A. J. 1989. "The Aesthetics of a Blood Sport." *Diogenes* (145): 46-58.

Aristotle. 1941. "Politics." In *The Basic Works of Aristotle*, 1127-1316. New York: Random House.

———. 1941. "Nicomachean Ethics." In *The Basic Works of Aristotle*, 935-1126. ed. Richard McKeon. New York: Random House.

Arseniev, V. K. 1941. *Dersu the Trapper.* New York: E. P. Dutton & Co., Inc.

Atkinson, Peter. 2009. *Making Game: An Essay on Hunting. Familiar Things, and the Strangeness of Being Who One Is.* Edmonton, Alberta: AU Press, Athabasca University.

Balon, E. K. 2000. "Defending Fishes Against Recreational Fishing: An Old Problem to be Solved in the New Millennium." *Environmental Biology of Fishes* 57 (1): 1-8.

Barnes, J. 1984. *The Complete Works of Aristotle.* 2 vols. Princeton: Princeton University Press.

Baron, David. 2004. *The Beast in the Garden.* New York: W. W. Norton & Company.

Bloomfield, Paul. 2000. "Virtue Epistemology and the Epistemology of Virtue." *Philosophy and Phenomenological Research* LX (1) (January): 23-43.

Borgmann, Albert. 1984. *Technology and the Character of Contemporary Life.* Chicago: University of Chicago Press.

Bronner, Simon. 2008. *Killing Tradition: Inside Hunting and Animal Rights Controversies.* Lexington: The University Press of Kentucky.

Brower, Matthew. 2011. *Developing Animals: Wildlife and Early American Photography.* Minneapolis: University of Minnesota Press.

Brown, Tommy L., Decker, Daniel J., and Kelley, John W. 1983. "Access to Private Lands for Hunting in New York: 1963-1980." *Wildlife Society Bulletin* 12 (4): 344-349.

Brown, W. Miller. 2002. "Practices and Prudence." In *Philosophy of Sport: Critical Readings, Crucial Issues*, 64-75. Upper Saddle River, New Jersey: Prentice Hall.

Budiansky, Stephen. 1992. *The Covenant of the Wild: Why Animals Chose Domestication*. New York: W. Morrow.

Burtt, Tony, and Tony Faast. 2002. "An Alternative View of Alternative Delivery in Hunter Education." *Journal of Hunter Education* (Winter): 12.

Cafaro, P. 1998. "Less Is More: Economic Consumption and the Good Life." *Philosophy Today* 42 (1): 26-39.

———. 2001. "Thoreau, Leopold, and Carson: Toward an Environmental Virtue Ethics." *Environmental Ethics* 22 (Spring): 3-17.

———. 2005. "Gluttony, Arrogance, Greed, and Apathy: An Exploration of Environmental Vice." In *Environmental Virtue Ethics*, 135-158. Lanham, Maryland: Rowman & Littlefield Publishers, Inc.

Callicott, B. J. 1989. *In Defense of the Land Ethic*. Albany: State University of New York.

———. 1997. "Whaling in Sand County: The Morality of Norwegian Minke Whale Catching." In *Philosophy of the Environment*, 156-179. Edinburgh: Edinburgh University Press.

Callicott, J. B. 1989. "Aldo Leopold on Education, as Educator, and His Land Ethic in the Context of Contemporary Environmental Education." In *In Defense of the Land Ethic: Essays in Environmental Philosophy*, 223-237. Albany, New York: SUNY Press.

Camuto, Christopher. 2001. *A Fly Fisherman's Blue Ridge*. University of Georgia Press.

Caras, R. 1970. *Death as a Way of Life*. Boston: Little Brown and Co.

Carr, D. 1999. "Where's the Merit if the Best Man Wins?" *Journal of the Philosophy of Sport* XXVI: 1-9.

Cartmill, M. 1993. *A View to a Death in the Morning: Hunting and Nature Through History*. Cambridge: Harvard University Press.

Causey, A. 1989. "On the Morality of Hunting." *Environmental Ethics* 11: 317-343.

Chipeniuk, R. 1997. "On Contemplating the Interests of Fish." *Environmental Ethics* 19 (3): 331-332.

Cohan, J. A. 2003. "Is Hunting a 'Sport?'" *International Journal of Applied Philosophy* 17 (2): 291-326.

Collard, Andree, and Joyce Contrucci. 1989. *Rape of the Wild: Man's Violence Against Animals and the Earth*. Bloomington: Indiana University Press.

Comstock, G. L. 2004. "Subsistence Hunting." In *Food for Thought: The Debate Over Eating Meat*, 359-371. ed. S. F. Sapontzis. Amherst: Prometheus Books.

Cooper, J. M. 1993. "Political Animals and Civic Friendship." In *Friendship: A Philosophical Reader*, ed. N.K. Badwar, 303-326. Ithaca: Cornell University Press.

Corlett, John. 2002. "Virtue Lost: Courage in Sport." In *Philosophy of Sport: Critical Readings, Crucial Issues*, ed. M. Andrew Holowchak, 454-465. Upper Saddle River, NJ: Prentice Hall.

Crawford, Matthew, B. 2009. *Shop Class as Soulcraft: An Inquiry Into the Value of Work*. New York: The Penguin Press.

Curnutt, J. 1996. "How to Argue For and Against Sport Hunting." *Journal of Social Philosophy* 27: 65-89.

Dahles, H. 1993. "Game Killing and Killing Games: An Anthropologist Looking at Hunting in a Modern Society." *Society and Animals* 1 (2): 169-184.

Disilvestro, Roger. 1989. *The Endangered Kingdom: The Struggle to Save America's Wildlife*. New York: Wiley.

Dizard, Jan E. 2003. *Mortal Stakes: Hunters and Hunting in Contemporary America*. Amherst: University of Massachusetts Press.

Dreyfus, H. I., and S. E. Dreyfus. 1990. "What is Morality? A Phenomenological Account of the Development of Ethical Expertise." In *Universalism vs. Communitarianism: Contemporary Debates in Ethics*, 237-264. Cambridge: The MIT Press.

Dunlap, Thomas. 1988. *Saving America's Wildlife*. Princeton: Princeton University Press.

Egan, Timothy. 2009. *The Big Burn: Teddy Roosevelt and the Fire that Saved America*. New York: Mariner Books.

Evans, J. Claude. 2005. *With Respect for Nature: Living as Part of the Natural World*. Albany: SUNY Press.

Everett, J. 2001. "Environmental Ethics, Animal Welfarism, and the Problem of Predation: A Bambi Lover's Respect for Nature." *Ethics & the Environment* 6 (1): 42-67.

Farrell, Sean Patrick. 2009. "The Urban Deerslayer." *New York Times*, November 24.

Flader, Susan. 2003. "Building Conservation on the Land: Aldo Leopold and the Tensions of Professionalism and Citizenship." In *Reconstructing Conservation: Finding Common Ground*, ed. Minteer, Ben and Robert Manning, 115-132. Washington, D.C.: Island Press.

Foster, S. E. 2002. "Aristotle and the Environment." *Environmental Ethics* 24 (4): 409-428.

Fox, Stephen. 1981. *The American Conservation Movement: John Muir and His Legacy*. Madison: The University of Wisconsin Press.

Frankena, William K. 1965. *Three Historical Philosophies of Education: Aristotle, Kant, and Dewey*. Atlanta: Scott, Foreman and Company.

Frasz, G. B. 1993. "Environmental Virtue Ethics: A New Direction for Environmental Ethics." *Environmental Ethics* 15 (3): 259-274.

———. 2001. "What Is Environmental Virtue Ethics That We Should Be Mindful Of It?" *Philosophy in the Contemporary World* 8 (2): 5-14.

Gaard, Greta, ed. 1993. *Ecofeminism: Women, Animals, and Nature*. Philadelphia: Temple University Press.

Gaard, Greta. 1993. "Ecofeminism and Native American Cultures." In *Ecofeminism: Women, Animals, and Nature*, 295-314. Philadelphia: Temple University Press.

Goff, G. 2002. *Ethics Training*. Cornell University, Ithaca, New York

Gray, Gary G. 1993. *Wildlife and People: The Human Dimension of Wildlife Ecology*. Chicago: University of Illinois Press.

de Grazia, Sebastian. 1962. *Of Time, Work, and Leisure*. Millwood, New York: Kraus International Publications.

Greenberg, Paul. 2010. *Four Fish: The Future of the Last Wild Food*. New York: The Penguin Press.

Gunn, A. S. 2001. "Environmental Ethics and Trophy Hunting." *Ethics & the Environment* 6 (1): 68-95.

Haig-Brown, Robert L. 1946. *A River Never Sleeps*. New York: Crown Publishers, Inc.

———. 2001. "Putting Fish Back." In *On Killing: Meditations On the Chase*, 87-93. Guilford, Connecticut: The Lyons Press.

Hamm, Dale, and David Bakke. 1996. *The Last of the Market Hunters*. Carbondale: Southern Illinois University Press.

Hammond, Bryn. 1994. *Halcyon Days: The Nature of Trout Fishing and Fishermen*. Camden, Maine: Ragged Mountain Press.

Hanna, Edward. 2007. "Fair Chase: To Where Does It Lead?" In *The Culture of Hunting in Canada*. ed. Jean L. Manore and Dale G. Miner, 239-261. Vancouver: UBC Press.

Hargrove, Eugene C. 1996. *Foundations of Environmental Ethics*. Denton, Texas: Environmental Ethics Books.

Hemingway, J. L. 1991. "Leisure and Democracy: Incompatible Ideals?" In *Leisure and Ethics: Reflections on the Philosophy of Leisure*, 59-81. Reston,

Virginia: American Alliance for Health, Physical Education, Recreation and Dance.

Herbert, Henry William. 1868. *Field Sports of the United States and British Provinces of North America.* 8th ed. Vol. 1. New York: W. A. Townsend & Adams.

Herman, Daniel. 2001. *Hunting and the American Imagination.* Washington, D.C.: Smithsonian Institution Press.

Hettinger, N. 1994. "Valuing Predation in Rolston's Environmental Ethics: Bambi Lovers versus Tree Huggers." *Environmental Ethics* 16: 3-20.

Hettinger, Ned. 2010. "Animal Beauty, Ethics, and Environmental Preservation." *Environmental Ethics* 32 (2): 115-134.

Hill, T. 2005. "Ideals of Human Excellence and Preserving Natural Environments." In *Environmental Virtue Ethics*, 47-59. Lanham, Maryland: Rowman & Littlefield Publishers, Inc.

Holly, Marilyn. 2006. "Environmental Virtue Ethics: A Review of Some Current Work." *Journal of Agriculture and Environmental Ethics* 19: 391-424.

Homiak, M. 2004. "Virtue and the Skills of Ordinary Life." In *Setting the Moral Compass: Essays by Women Philosophers*, ed. C. Calhoun, 23-42. New York: Oxford University Press.

Howe, L.A. 2008. "Remote Sport: Risk and Self-knowledge in Wilder Spaces." *Journal of the Philosophy of Sport* 35 (1): 1-16.

Hull, Robert. 2005. "All About EVE: A Report on Environmental Virtue Ethics Today." *Ethics & the Environment* 10 (1): 89-110.

Jacobson, D. 2005. "Seeing By Feeling: Virtues, Skills, and Moral Perception." *Ethical Theory and Moral Practice*: 387-409.

Jensen, J. 2001. "The Virtues of Hunting." *Philosophy in the Contemporary World.* (Fall-Winter, 2): 113-124.

Jolma, Dena Jones. 1992. *Hunting Quotations.* Jefferson, North Carolina: MacFarland & Company, Inc.

Jones, A.M. 1997a. "Heart of the Hunt." In *On Killing: Meditations on the Chase*, 165-174. Guilford, Connecticut: The Lyons Press.

———. 1997b. *A Quiet Place of Violence: Hunting and Ethics in the Missouri River Breaks.* Bozeman, Montana: Spring Creek Publishing.

Jones, Robert F. 2001. *On Killing: Meditations On the Chase.* Guilford, Connecticut: The Lyons Press.

Kalinowski, F. A. 1996. "Aldo Leopold as Hunter and Communitarian." In *Rooted In the Land: Essays on Community and Place*, 140-149. New Haven: Yale University Press.

Kellert, S.R. 1978. "Attitudes and Characteristics of Hunters and Anti-Hunters and Related Policy Suggestions." In *Transactions of the North American Wildlife and Natural Resources Conference*.

Kerasote, Ted. 1993. *Bloodties: Nature, Culture, and the Hunt*. New York: Random House.

————. 1997. *Heart of Home*. New York: Villard.

Kessler, W. B., and A. L. Booth. 2002. "Professor Leopold, What Is Education For?" In *Aldo Leopold and the Ecological Conscience*, 118-127. New York: Oxford University Press.

Kheel, M. 1995. "License to Kill: An Ecofeminist Critique of Hunter's Discourse." In *Animals and Women*, 85-125. Durham: Duke University Press.

Kheel, M. 1996. "The Killing Game: An Ecofeminist Critique of Hunting." *Journal of the Philosophy of Sport* 23: 30-44.

King, R. 1991. "Environmental Ethics and the Case for Hunting." *Environmental Ethics* 13: 59-85.

Knight, R. L., S. Riedel, and S. Riedel. 2002. *Aldo Leopold and the Ecological Conscience*. New York: Oxford University Press.

Kowalsky, Nathan. 2010. *Hunting—Philosophy for Everyone: In Search of the Wild Life*. Malden, Massachusetts: Wiley-Blackwell.

Kraut, Richard. 1991. *Aristotle on the Human Good*. Princeton: Princeton University Press.

Laney, Dawn, ed. 2008. *Hunting*. Farmington Hills, Michigan: Greenhaven Press.

Leeuw, A.D. 1996. "Contemplating the Interests of Fish." *Environmental Ethics* 18 (4): 373-390.

————. 1998. "The Interests of Fish: Reply to Chipaniuk (Sic) and List." *Environmental Ethics* 20 (2): 219-220.

————. 2004. "Angling and Sadism: a Response to Olsen." *Environmental Ethics* 26 (4): 441-42.

Leopold, Aldo. 1966. *A Sand County Almanac with Essays on Conservation from Round River*. New York: Ballantine Books.

————. 1999. "The Outlook for Farm Wildlife." In *For the Health of the Land*, 213-218. Washington, D.C.: Island Press.

————. 1986. *Game Management*. Madison: The University of Wisconsin Press.

————. 1991a. "Land Pathology." In *The River of the Mother of God and Other Essays*, ed. Susan L. Flader and J. Baird Callicott, 212-217. Madison: University of Wisconsin Press.

———. 1991b. "The Conservation Ethic." In *The River of the Mother of God and Other Essays*, 181-192.

———. 1991c. "Game and Wild Life Conservation." In *The River of the Mother of God and Other Essays*, 164-168.

———. 1991d. "The Ecological Conscience." In *The River of the Mother of God and Other Essays*, 338-346.

———. 1991e. "Means and Ends in Wild Life Management." In *The River of the Mother of God and Other Essays*, 235-238.

Light, A. 2004. "Methodological Pragmatism, Animal Welfare, and Hunting." In *Animal Pragmatism: Rethinking Human-Nonhuman Relationships*, 119-139. Bloomington: Indiana University Press.

List, C. 1997a. "Is Hunting a Right Thing?" *Environmental Ethics* 18: 405-416.

———. 1997b. "On Angling as an Act of Cruelty." *Environmental Ethics* 19 (3): 333-334.

———. 1998. "On the Moral Significance of a Hunting Ethic." *Ethics & the Environment* 3 (2): 157-175.

———. 1999. "Guiding Outdoor Recreation Toward the Land Ethic." *Adirondack Journal of Environmental Studies* 6 (2): 8-10.

———. 2004. "On the Moral Distinctiveness of Sport Hunting." *Environmental Ethics* 26 (2): 155-169.

———. 2005. "The Virtues of Wild Leisure." *Environmental Ethics* 27 (4): 355-373.

Loo, Tina. 2006. *States of Nature: Conserving Canada's Wildlife in the Twentieth Century*. Vancouver: UBC Press.

Lord, Carnes. 1982. *Education and Culture in the Political Thought of Aristotle*. Ithaca: Cornell University Press.

Louv, Richard. 2008. *Last Child in the Woods: Saving Our Children from Nature-Deficit Disorder*. Chapel Hill: Algonquin Books of Chapel Hill.

Luce, A. A. 1959. *Fishing and Thinking*. Camden, Maine: Ragged Mountain Press.

Luke, B. 1997. "A Critical Analysis of Hunter's Ethics." *Environmental Ethics* 19: 25-44.

Lyons, Nick. 2009. "Thomas McGuane: A Profile." *Fly Rod & Reel*, January.

MacIntyre, Alasdair. 1981. *After Virtue: A Study in Moral Theory*. Notre Dame: University of Notre Dame Press.

Mallory, C. 2001. "Acts of Objectification and the Repudiation of Dominance: Leopold, Ecofeminism, and the Ecological Narrative." *Ethics & the Environment* 6 (2): 59-89.

Manore, Jean, and Dale Miner, eds. 2007. *The Culture of Hunting in Canada.* Vancouver: UBC Press.

Marriner, Paul. 2009. "Czech-Style Nymphing: Learning the Art of Trout Touch." *Fly Fisherman*, 41 (May): 44f.

Matthews, Bruce, and Cheryl Riley. 1995. *Teaching and Evaluating Outdoor Ethics Education Programs.* National Wildlife Federation.

McPhee, John. 2002. *The Founding Fish.* New York: Farrar, Straus and Giroux.

Mighetto, Lisa. 1991. *Wild Animals and American Environmental Ethics.* Tucson: University of Arizona Press.

Moline, Jon. 1986. "Aldo Leopold and the Moral Community." *Environmental Ethics* 8: 99-120.

Momaday, N. Scott. 1998. "A First American's View." In *Environmental Ethics: Divergence and Convergence*, 252-256. Boston: McGraw Hill.

Moriarty, P.V., and M. Woods. 1997. "Hunting [Is Not Identical to] Predation." *Environmental Ethics* 19: 391-404.

Nelson, Michael. 2010. "Teaching Holism in Environmental Ethics." *Environmental Ethics* 32 (1): 33-50.

Newton, Julianne Lutz. 2006. *Aldo Leopold's Odyssey: Rediscovering the Author of A Sand County Almanac.* Washington, D.C.: Island Press/Shearwater Books.

Nussbaum, Martha C. 1999. "The Discernment of Perception: An Aristotelian Conception of Private and Public Rationality." In *Aristotle's Ethics: Critical Essays*, 145-182. Lanham, Maryland: Rowman & Littlefield Publishers, Inc.

———. 2002. "Non-Relative Virtues." In *Moral Relativism: A Reader*, ed. Paul K. Moser and Thomas L. Carson, 199-225. New York: Oxford University Press.

———. 2006. *Frontiers of Justice: Disability, Nationality, Species Membership.* Cambridge, Massachusetts: The Belknap Press.

O'Neill, J. 1993. *Ecology, Policy and Politics: Human Well-Being and the Natural World.* London: Routledge.

Olsen, Len. 2003. "Contemplating the Intentions of Anglers: The Ethicist's Challenge." *Environmental Ethics* 25 (3): 267-277.

Ortega y Gasset, J. 1995. *Meditations on Hunting.* Bozeman, Montana: Wilderness Adventure Press.

Ouderkirk, W., and J. Hill, eds. 2002. *Land, Value, Community: Callicott and Environmental Philosophy.* Albany: SUNY Press.

Palmer, Clair, and Francis O'Gorman. 2003. "Animals, Power and Ethics: The Case of Foxhunting." In *Moral and Political Reasoning in Environmental Practice*, ed. A. Light and Avner de-Shalit, 281-294. Cambridge, Massachusetts: The MIT Press.

Parsons, Glenn. 2008. *Aesthetics and Nature.* London: Continuum International Publishing Group.

Pauley, J. A. 2003. "The Value of Hunting." *Journal of Value Inquiry* 37 (2): 233-244.

Petersen, D. 2000. *Heartsblood: Hunting, Spirituality, and Wildness In America.* Washington, D.C.: Island Press/Shearwater Books.

Peterson, M. Nils. 2004. "An Approach for Demonstrating the Social Legitimacy of Hunting." *Wildlife Society Bulletin* 32 (2): 310-321.

Pimentel, David, Laura Westra, and Reed F. Noss. 2000. *Ecological Integrity: Integrating Environment, Conservation, and Health.* Washington, D.C.: Island Press.

Van de Pitte, Margaret. 2003. "The Moral Basis for Public Policy Encouraging Sport Hunting." *Journal of Social Philosophy* 34 (2): 256-266.

Plato. 1961. "Laws." In *Plato: The Collected Dialogues*, 1225-1513. ed. Edith Hamilton and Huntington Cairns. Princeton: Princeton University Press.

———. "Sophist." In *Plato: The Collected Dialogues*, 957-1017. ed. Edith Hamilton and Huntington Cairns. Princeton: Princeton University Press.

Pohl, S. 2006. "Technology and the Wilderness Experience." *Environmental Ethics* 28 (2): 147-163.

Pollan, Michael. 1991. *Second Nature: A Gardener's Education.* New York: Grove Press.

———. 2006. *The Omnivore's Dilemma: A Natural History of Four Meals.* New York: The Penguin Press.

Posewitz, Jim. 1994. *Beyond Fair Chase: The Ethic and Tradition of Hunting.* Helena, Montana: Falcon.

———. 1999. *Inherit the Hunt: A Journey into the Heart of American Hunting.* Guilford, Connecticut: TwoDot.

Rabb, J. D. 2002. "The Vegetarian Fox and Indigenous Philosophy: Speciesism, Racism, and Sexism." *Environmental Ethics* 24 (3): 275-294.

Rawls, John. 1971. *A Theory of Justice.* Cambridge: Harvard University Press.

Regan, Tom. 1983. *The Case for Animal Rights.* Berkeley: University of California Press.

Reiger, John. 2001. *American Sportsmen and the Origin of Conservation.* 3rd ed. Corvallis: Oregon State University Press.

Rolston III, Holmes. 1988. *Environmental Ethics: Duties To and Values In the Natural World.* Philadelphia: Temple University Press.

Roochnik, David. 1996. *Of Art and Wisdom: Plato's Understanding of Techne.* University Park: The Pennsylvania State University Press.

Roosevelt, Theodore. 1996. *Hunting Trips of a Ranchman & The Wilderness Hunter.* New York: The Modern Library.

Sandler, Ronald, and Philip Cafaro. 2005. *Environmental Virtue Ethics.* Lanham, Maryland: Rowman & Littlefield Publishers, Inc.

Sapontzis, Steve F. 1987. *Morals, Reason, and Animals.* Philadelphia: Temple University Press.

Sax, Joseph. 1980. *Mountains Without Handrails: Reflection on the National Parks.* Ann Arbor: The University of Michigan Press.

Scheck, Art. 2003. "Breakfast Decisions." In *A Fishing Life is Hard Work,* 109-118. Mechanicsburg, Pennsylvania: Stackpole Books.

Schwartz, Barry, and Kenneth Sharpe. 2010. *Practical Wisdom: The Right Way to Do the Right Thing.* New York: Riverhead Books.

Scruton, R. 1997. "From a View to a Death: Culture, Nature and the Huntsman's Art." *Environmental Values* 6 (4): 471-481.

———. 2002. "Ethics and Welfare: the Case of Hunting." *Philosophy: the Journal of the British Institute of Philosophical Studies* 77 (October): 543-64.

Shaw, B. 1997. "A Virtue Ethics Approach to Aldo Leopold's Land Ethic." *Environmental Ethics* 19: 53-67.

Shepard, Paul. 1973. *The Tender Carnivore and the Sacred Game.* Athens: University of Georgia Press.

Sherman, Nancy. 1999. "The Habituation of Character." In *Aristotle's Ethics: Critical Essays,* 231-260. Lanham, Maryland: Rowman & Littlefield Publishers, Inc.

Shivers, Jay. 1981. *Leisure and Recreation Concepts: A Critical Analysis.* Boston: Allyn and Bacon Inc.

Stanford, Craig B. 1999. *The Hunting Apes: Meat Eating and the Origins of Human Behavior.* Princeton: Princeton University Press.

Stanford, Sue P. 2010. "Intellectual Virtue in Environmental Virtue Ethics." *Environmental Ethics* 32 (4): 339-352.

Stange, Mary Zeiss. 1997. *Woman the Hunter.* Boston: Beacon Press.

Swan, James A. 1995. *In Defense of Hunting.* San Francisco: Harper.

Swanson, Judith Ann. 1992. *The Public and the Private in Aristotle's Political Philosophy.* Ithaca: Cornell University Press.

Tantillo, J. 2001. "Sport Hunting, Eudaimonia, and Tragic Wisdom." *Philosophy in the Contemporary World* 8 (2): 101-112.

Tiles, J. E. 1984. "Techne and Moral Expertise." *Philosophy: The Journal of the British Institute of Philosophical Studies* 59: 49-66.

Tober, James A. 1981. *Who Owns the Wildlife?* Westport, Conneticut: Greenwood Press.

Valdene, Guy. 1995. *For a Handful of Feathers.* New York: The Atlantic Monthly Press.

van Wensveen, Louke. 2000. *Dirty Virtues: The Emergence of Ecological Virtue Ethics.* Amherst, New York: Humanity Books.

Varner, Gary E. 1995. Can Animal Rights Activists Be Environmentalists? In *Environmental Philosophy and Environmental Activism*, 169-201. Lanham, Maryland: Rowman & Littlefield Publishers.

Vitali, T. 1990. "Sport Hunting: Moral Or Immoral?" *Environmental Ethics* 12: 69-82.

Wade, M. L. 1990. "Animal Liberationism, Ecocentrism, and the Morality of Sport Hunting." *Journal of the Philosophy of Sport* 17: 15-27.

Wallace, J. D. 1974. "Excellences and Merit." *The Philosophical Review* 83 (2) (April): 182-199.

———. 1988. "Ethics and the Craft Analogy." *Midwest Studies in Philosophy*: 222-232.

Walton, Izaak. *The Compleat Angler.* http://www.gutenberg.org/dirs/etext96/tcang10.txt.

Warren, Louis S. 1997. *The Hunter's Game: Poachers and Conservationists in Twentieth-Century America.* New Haven: Yale University Press.

Washabaugh, William, and Catherine Washabaugh. 2000. *Deep Trout: Angling in Popular Culture.* New York: Berg.

Wenz, Peter S. 1995. Environmental Activism and Appropriate Monism. In *Environmental Philosophy and Environmental Activism*, 215-227. Lanham, Maryland: Rowman & Littlefield Publishers.

Westra, Laura, and T.M. Robinson. 1997. *The Greeks and the Environment.* Lanham, Maryland: Rowman & Littlefield Publishers.

Wick, W. 1971. "The Rat and the Squirrel, or The Rewards of Virtue." *Ethics* 82 (1) (October): 21-32.

Williams, Joy. 1995. "The Killing Game." In *Women On Hunting*, 248-265. Hopewell, New Jersey: The Ecco Press.

Wonders, Karen. 2005. "Hunting Narratives of the Age of Empire: A Gender Reading of their Iconography." *Environment and History* 11 (3): 269-291.

Wood Jr., Forrest. 1997. *The Delights and Dilemmas of Hunting: The Hunting versus Anti-Hunting Debate.* Lanham, Maryland: University Press of America.

Worster, Donald. 1979. *Nature's Economy: The Roots of Ecology.* Garden City, New York: Anchor Books.

Zagzebski, Linda Trinkaus. 1996. *Virtues of the Mind: An Inquiry into the Nature of Virtue and the Ethical Foundations of Knowledge.* Cambridge: Cambridge University Press.

ENDNOTES

PART ONE

Chapter One

1   He interestingly eliminates all kinds of fishing and any hunting with nets or traps as unworthy of his young athletes.

2   Plato, "Laws," in *Plato: The Collected Dialogues*, ed. Edith Hamilton and Huntington Cairns (Princeton: Princeton University Press, 1961). 824b.

3   Daniel Herman, *Hunting and the American Imagination* (Washington, D.C.: Smithsonian Institution Press, 2001). Herman traces the remarkably variable historical career of the sportsmanship thesis from the American Revolution until about 1900. His interest is in the historical and cultural factors responsible for developing what he calls the image of the "American Native" best illustrated by Daniel Boone, Davy Crockett, and eventually Teddy Roosevelt. It is interesting to note that Herman makes a persuasive case that public doubts about the social acceptability of hunting lifted briefly after the Revolutionary War and in a more sustained way after the Civil War. It became a popular belief that the most successful soldiers in each war were those trained in youth by hunting.

4   Izaak Walton, *The Compleat Angler*, n.d., 27, http://www.gutenberg. org/dirs/etext96/tcang10.txt.

5   Cited by John F. Reiger, *American Sportsmen and the Origins of Conservation*, third edition. (Corvallis: Oregon State University Press, 2001), 48, by an anonymous author.

6   Herman, *Hunting and the American Imagination*. "Hunting promoted the internalization of virtue demanded by middle-class life; hunting taught "self-possession, self-control, and promptness in execution," "patience," "perseverance," "sagacity," and "knowledge of human nature." 105.

    This list of virtues is taken from John Mason Peck, a minister, in his hagiography of Daniel Boone.

7   *Today's Hunter: A Guide to Hunting Responsibly and Safely*, Northeast. (Dallas, TX: Kalkomey Enterprises, 2009). 71.

8   Theodore Roosevelt, *Hunting Trips of a Ranchman & The Wilderness Hunter* (New York: The Modern Library, 1996). 348.

9   David Roochnik, *Of Art and Wisdom: Plato's Understanding of Techne* (University Park, Pennsylvania: The Pennsylvania State University Press, 1996). 90.

10 Ibid., 91. There is a large literature devoted to the evaluation of arguments designed to close this gap. Some of this will play a role in the next chapter.

11 Herman, *Hunting and the American Imagination* 65. There is an interesting backstory here told by Herman. In 1790, the activity that won high marks for virtue development was farming. In agriculture one made the land into one's property, as Locke argued. Hunting was seen as idleness; food could be had without much work. For the American pioneers, this looked too much like the life of the natives they were fervently trying to supplant. But just a hundred years later, hunting, not farming, won praise for inculcating virtue. This remarkable turn of events is well documented by Herman, but my interests lay in the general soundness of the sportsman thesis and not in its historical career.

12 Roosevelt, *Hunting Trips of a Ranchman & The Wilderness Hunter.* 329.

13 At this point it is appropriate for me to explain my subsequent use of the term "sportsman." The virtues I argue for are not "manly" nor are the intended to be so. The exclusionary version of the sportsman thesis has no place in my argument, and even though I shall continue to refer to "sportsmen" I mean sportswomen too.

Chapter Two

1   See H. I. Dreyfus and S. E. Dreyfus, "What is Morality? A Phenomenological Account of the Development of Ethical Expertise," in *Universalism vs. Communitarianism: Contemporary Debates in Ethics* (Cambridge: The MIT Press, 1990), 237-64; D. Jacobson, "Seeing By Feeling: Virtues, Skills, and Moral Perception," *Ethical Theory and Moral Practice* (2005): 387-409; J. E. Tiles, "Techne and Moral Expertise," *Philosophy: the Journal of the British Institute of Philosophical Studies* 59 (JA 1984): 49-66.

2   Animals of the "right sort" are game animals, a concept I will explore in Chapter Thirteen.

3   See J. O'Neill, *Ecology, Policy and Politics: Human Well-Being and the Natural World* (London: Routledge, 1993). "Practical knowledge requires capacities of judgment and perception of particular cases that can be learned only by habituation and which cannot, like technical knowledge, be found in books." 125.

4   It is, of course, possible to learn to do an activity by oneself, without the guidance of instructors. Indeed, much of the practice may occur in isolation. But for one to participate in an activity one must become aware of the standards and their histories.

5   For an interesting comparison see Matthew Crawford B., *Shop Class as Soulcraft: An Inquiry Into the Value of Work* (New York: The Penguin Press, 2009).

6   Paul Bloomfield, "Virtue Epistemology and the Epistemology of Virtue," *Philosophy and Phenomenological Research* LX, no. 1 (January 2000): 23-43. Also Jacobson, "Seeing By Feeling: Virtues, Skills, and Moral Perception."

7   For a popular introduction to this see: Barry Schwartz and Kenneth Sharpe, *Practical Wisdom: The Right Way to Do the Right Thing* (New York: Riverhead Books, 2010).

8   Bloomfield, "Virtue Epistemology and the Epistemology of Virtue."

9   Paul Marriner, "Czech-Style Nymphing: Learning the Art of Trout Touch," *Fly Fisherman*, 2009.

10   N. Sherman, "The Habituation of Character," in *Aristotle's Ethics: Critical Essays* (Lanham: Rowman & Littlefield Publishers, Inc., 1999), 231-60. "The Aristotelian presupposition is that the ability to discriminate is already there and in evidence [in children] as is an interest and a delight in improvement. What is required is a shifting of beliefs and perspectives through the guidance of an outside instructor. Such guidance cannot merely be a matter of bringing the child to see this way now, but of providing some sort of continuous and consistent instruction which will allow for the formation of patterns and trends in what the child notices and sees." 242.

11   ". . . in stochastic technai things do not entirely come about according to what the techne is for the sake of. And the cause of this is that they come about by chance and the methods through which the things coming about from these techai actually come about are not well defined." Alexander quoted by Roochnik, *Of Art and Wisdom: Plato's Understanding of Techne*, 55.

12   Crawford, *Shop Class as Soulcraft: An Inquiry Into the Value of Work*, 27. Compare this to what Bloomfield says: "diagnosis proceeds by the 'reading' of signs and symptoms: abduction is performed from the inferential basis of the signs to their underlying causes." 29.

13   Bryn Hammond, *Halcyon Days: The Nature of Trout Fishing and Fishermen* (Camden, Maine: Ragged Mountain Press, 1994). Hammond, in the chapter "Fisherman's Luck," goes so far as to speculate on some extra-sensory sixth sense enjoyed by certain extremely successful anglers.

Chapter Three

1   See Bloomfield, "Virtue Epistemology and the Epistemology of Virtue." Also J. Annas, "Virtue as a Skill," *International Journal of Philosophical Studies* 3, no. 2 (1995): 227-43.

2   See for instance M. C. Nussbaum, "The Discernment of Perception: An Aristotelian Conception of Private and Public Rationality," in *Aristotle's Ethics: Critical Essays* (Lanham: Rowman & Littlefield Publishers, Inc., 1999), 145-82. J. D. Wallace, "Ethics and the Craft Analogy," *Midwest Studies in Philosophy* (1988): 222-32. L. T. Zagzebski, *Virtues of the Mind: An Inquiry into the Nature of Virtue and the Ethical Foundations of Knowledge* (Cambridge: Cambridge University Press, 1996).

3   Ibid., 137.

4   In Part Two I will take up the issue of what this end might be for field sports.

5   J. Barnes, *The Complete Works of Aristotle* (Princeton: Princeton University Press, 1984), Nicomachean Ethics 1103b20-26.

6   In some happy cases one may find it possible to work at something one would do for its own sake anyway.

7   J. A. Swanson, *The Public and the Private in Aristotle's Political Philosophy* (Ithaca: Cornell University Press, 1992), 159.

8   Carnes Lord. *Education and Culture in the Political Thought of Aristotle*, Ithaca: Cornell University Press, 1982, 150. Unfortunately, while I am arguing that Aristotle's view supports this, it is also clear that for Aristotle himself, hunting and angling are not leisure activities in the required sense, because Aristotle consistently views them as activities done for the sake of providing food.

9   Aristotle, Politics, bk. VII, chap. 5, 1340a6. See Lord, *Education and Culture in the Political Thought of Aristotle*, 74.

10   Ibid. 103. See also Swanson. *The Public and the Private in Aristotle's Political Philosophy*. 151-54.

11   J. Rawls, *A Theory of Justice* (Cambridge: Harvard University Press, 1971), 426.

12   Activities such as these are "practices" in MacIntyre's sense. See A. MacIntyre, *After Virtue: A Study in Moral Theory* (Notre Dame: University of Notre Dame Press, 1981).

13   See Annas' comments on the paucity of virtue development in sport. Annas, "Virtue as a Skill." Contrast W. Miller Brown, "Practices and Prudence," in *Philosophy of Sport: Critical Readings, Crucial Issues* (Upper Saddle River, NJ: Prentice Hall, 2002), 69.

14 See Zagzebski, *Virtues of the Mind: An Inquiry into the Nature of Virtue and the Ethical Foundations of Knowledge.*

15 M. Homiak, "Virtue and the Skills of Ordinary Life," in *Setting the Moral Compass: Essays by Women Philosophers*, ed. C. Calhoun (New York: Oxford University Press, 2004), 23-42.

16 Ibid., 34.

17 As we'll see, once the community is expanded to become the "biotic community," the virtues required take on a distinctly ecological form.

18 Homiak, "Virtue and the Skills of Ordinary Life." 30.

19 Bloomfield, "Virtue Epistemology and the Epistemology of Virtue."

20 Aristotle, *Nicomachean Ethics* (1109b23).

21 For more on these ideas see C. J. List, "The Virtues of Wild Leisure," *Environmental Ethics* 27, no. 4 (2005): 355-73.

PART TWO

1 B. Shaw, "A Virtue Ethics Approach to Aldo Leopold's Land Ethic," *Environmental Ethics* 19 (1997): 53-67; C. J. List, "The Virtues of Wild Leisure"; P. Cafaro, "Thoreau, Leopold, and Carson: Toward an Environmental Virtue Ethics," *Environmental Ethics* 22, spring (2001): 3-17; J. Jensen, "The Virtues of Hunting," *Philosophy in the Contemporary World* 8, no. 2 (2001): 113-24.

2 Louke van Wensveen, *Dirty Virtues: The Emergence of Ecological Virtue Ethics* (Amherst, New York: Humanity Books, 2000).

3 For the original statement of these three questions see W. K. Frankena, *Three Historical Philosophies of Education: Aristotle, Kant and Dewey* (Atlanta: Scott, Foresman and Company, 1965).

Chapter Four

1 For an interesting take on this see: Timothy Egan, *The Big Burn: Teddy Roosevelt and the Fire that Saved America* (New York: Mariner Books, 2009).

2 See Reiger, *American Sportsmen and the Origins of Conservation.*

3 Aldo Leopold, "The Conservation Ethic," in *The River of the Mother of God and Other Essays*, eds. Susan L. Flader and J. Baird Callicott (Madison: University of Wisconsin Press, 1991), 181-92.

4 Ibid. It should also be noted that in the restrictions on when and where animals might be taken there were many attempts to preserve habitat.

5   Reiger, *American Sportsmen and the Origins of Conservation*. See also
     L. S. Warren, *The Hunter's Game: Poachers and Conservationist in
     Twentieth-Century America* (New Haven, CT: Yale University Press,
     1997); Dale Hamm and David Bakke, *The Last of the Market Hunters*
     (Carbondale: Southern Illinois University Press, 1996).

6   T. R. Dunlap, *Saving America's Wildlife* (Princeton: Princeton
     University Press, 1988).

7   Herman, *Hunting and the American Imagination*. 105

8   See the important third edition Epilogue of Reiger, *American Sportsmen
     and the Origins of Conservation*.

9   There is an interesting and complex history of conservation between
     Teddy Roosevelt's views and Leopold's innovation. See Stephen
     Fox, *The American Conservation Movement: John Muir and His Legacy*
     (Madison: University of Wisconsin Press, 1981), chap. 6.

10   Julianne Lutz Newton, *Aldo Leopold's Odyssey: Rediscovering the Author
     of A Sand County Almanac* (Washington, D.C.: Island Press/Shearwater
     Books, 2006).

11   Aldo Leopold, "Land Pathology," in *The River of the Mother of God and
     Other Essays*, 212-17.

12   Herman, *Hunting and the American Imagination*. "From the vantage
     point of the twenty-first century, it is easy to see how limited the
     vision of these hunter-conservationists was. They might wish to save
     the buffalo and elk but not the Great Plains biome on which buffalo
     and elk thrived." 243.

13   Aldo Leopold, "The Conservation Ethic," 190.

Chapter Five

1   Aldo Leopold, *A Sand County Almanac with Essays on Conservation from
     Round River* (New York: Ballantine Books, 1966). 262.

2   For the complete argument see C. List, "Is Hunting a Right Thing?,"
     Environmental Ethics 18 (1997): 405-16.

3   A. Leopold, "The Ecological Conscience," in *The River of the
     Mother of God and Other Essays*. 345.

4   A. Leopold, *A Sand County Almanac with Essays on Conservation from
     Round River*. 199.

5   See David Pimentel, Laura Westra, and Reed F. Noss, *Ecological
     Integrity: Integrating Environment, Conservation, and Health* (Washington,
     D.C.: Island Press, 2000).

6   A. Leopold, *A Sand County Almanac with Essays on Conservation from Round River*. 247.

7   R. L. Knight and S. Riedel, *Aldo Leopold and the Ecological Conscience* (New York: Oxford University Press, 2002). See also Glenn Parsons, *Aesthetics and Nature* (London: Continuum International Pub., 2008).

8   A. Leopold, *A Sand County Almanac with Essays on Conservation from Round River*. "The taste for country displays the same diversity in aesthetic competence among individuals as the taste for opera, or oils." 179.

9   Note that diversity is not a measure of plentitude of species but general health of the biotic community.

10 A. Leopold, *A Sand County Almanac with Essays on Conservation from Round River*. 262.

11 Ibid. 251.

12 Ibid. 252.

13 M. L. Wade, "Animal Liberationism, Ecocentrism, and the Morality of Sport Hunting," *Journal of the Philosophy of Sport* 17 (1990) asks these critical questions but fails to see an answer.

14 Cf. S. F. Sapontzis, *Morals, Reason, and Animals* (Philadelphia: Temple University Press, 1987). He says that "it is far from obvious that the environment can properly be described as a 'community' in a morally significant sense." 266. Sapontzis uses this claim as evidence that Leopold's land ethic lacks "moral significance." Sapontzis mistakenly classifies the land ethic as a moral theory in and of itself. But the land ethic falls outside the moral expectations harbored by Sapontzis. It promotes, instead, a morality of character, virtue, and moral dispositions with regard to environmental practices.

Chapter Six

1   For a full analysis of these concepts derived from Leopold see C. J. List, "The Virtues of Wild Leisure." Note that I use "aesthetic" in the broad sense of concerning emotions and sensations.

2   For example, the kind of farm run by Joel Saladin, the Polyface Farm, is a result of all of the virtues I am discussing. See Michael Pollan, *The Omnivore's Dilemma: A Natural History of Four Meals* (New York: The Penguin Press, 2006).

3   A. Leopold, *A Sand County Almanac with Essays on Conservation from Round River*. Leopold asserts that developing an ecological conscience requires "an internal change in our intellectual emphasis, loyalties, affections, and convictions." 246.

4   Ibid., 258-59.

5   Aldo Leopold, "The Ecological Conscience," in *The River of the Mother of God and Other Essays*, 345.

6   J. Posewitz, *Beyond Fair Chase: The Ethic and Tradition of Hunting* (Helena, Montana: Falcon, 1994). I believe the ethical view I am developing here explains the need to go "beyond fair chase." This is yet another evolution of the sportsman thesis. I critically examine this doctrine, as well as stocking, in Part Three.

7   For a full analysis of how field sports must be redirected to affect this balance, see Chapter Eleven.

8   M. Kheel, "License to Kill: An Ecofeminist Critique of Hunter's Discourse," in *Animals and Women* (Durham: Duke University Press, 1995), 85-125. Kheel offers a critical evaluation of this virtue. See also J. C. Evans, *With Respect for Nature: Living as Part of the Natural World* (Albany: SUNY Press, 2005); Jensen, "The Virtues of Hunting."

9   A. Leopold, *A Sand County Almanac with Essays on Conservation from Round River*, 202.

10 Tina Loo, *States of Nature: Conserving Canada's Wildlife in the Twentieth Century* (Vancouver: UBC Press, 2006), 213. Loo, in discussing the extremes present in Canadian conservation thinking, says "Bureaucrats . . . justified their policies by appealing to the neutrality and authority of science. . . . Preservationists . . . asserted the disinterested authority of nature, the idea that, left to its own devices, nature would balance itself."

11 V. K. Arseniev, *Dersu the Trapper* (New York: E. P. Dutton & Co., Inc., 1941).

12 Martha C. Nussbaum, *Frontiers of Justice: Disability, Nationality, Species Membership* (Cambridge, MA: The Belknap Press, 2006).

13 A. Leopold, *A Sand County Almanac with Essays on Conservation from Round River*. 220.

14 Ibid. 205. See also Winnifred B. Kessler and Annie L. Booth, "Professor Leopold, What Is Education For?" in *Aldo Leopold and the Ecological Conscience*, eds. Richard L. Knight and Suzanne Riedel (New York: Oxford University Press, 2002), 118-27.

15 O'Neill, *Ecology, Policy and Politics: Human Well-Being and the Natural World*. "At the level of the development of habits and capacities there *is* a relation between science and value. The practice of science develops not just intellectual virtues but also ethical virtues. It is through the sciences, the arts and kindred practices that an appreciation of the intrinsic value of the natural world is developed." 162. See also

Fox, *The American Conservation Movement: John Muir and His Legacy.* Fox explores the concept of the amateur naturalist and its powerful influence in conservation.

16 See for instance R. Haig-Brown, *A River Never Sleeps* (New York: Crown Publishers, Inc., 1946); Christopher Camuto, *A Fly Fisherman's Blue Ridge* (Athens: University of Georgia Press, 2001).

17 For a thorough examination of the natural connections pursued by hunters see Guy de la Valdene, *For a Handful of Feathers* (New York: The Atlantic Monthly Press, 1995).

18 A. Leopold, *A Sand County Almanac with Essays on Conservation from Round River*, 290.

19 See a similar distinction in Ned Hettinger, "Animal Beauty, Ethics, and Environmental Preservation," *Environmental Ethics* 32, no. 2 (2010): 115-34. He says " . . . our aesthetic sense is not an isolated compartment of our lives but rather is fundamentally tied with who we are, what we believe, and what we value (including ethical value)." 130.

20 A. Leopold, *A Sand County Almanac with Essays on Conservation from Round River*, 179. My emphasis.

21 His discussion in "The Round River" and "Natural History" moves from his despair over the current state of biological education to his hope for the promotion of "amateur scholarship in the natural history field." See Donald Worster. *Nature's Economy: The Roots of Ecology* (Garden City, NY: Anchor Books, 1979). See also W. B. Kessler, and A. L. Booth. "Professor Leopold, What Is Education For? " in *Aldo Leopold and the Ecological Conscience* and Julianne Newton, *Aldo Leopold's Odyssey: Rediscovering the Author of A Sand County Almanac*, 270f.

22 A. Leopold, *A Sand County Almanac with Essays on Conservation from Round River*, 290.

23 Sherman. "The Habituation of Character," 238. A general account of the development of perceptual discernment as part of the education of desires may be found in Aristotle. How does Aristotle suggest we change or educate our affections or desires? Nancy Sherman, in discussing Aristotle's answer to this question says, " . . . emotions will be educated, in part, through their constitutive beliefs and perceptions." She goes on to say that this "cultivation of discriminatory abilities" or perceptual faculties is "included as part of habituation." For Aristotle, different parts of the soul respond to different kinds of education. The moral virtues, as capacities of the non-rational,

are educated primarily by habituation and the intellectual virtues, as capacities of the rational part of the soul, are swayed by argumentation. Habituation for Aristotle, then, is a matter of modifying passions by practicing the right arts under the guidance of instructors who can call one's attention to details unseen before. He says that we should pay close attention to people of practical wisdom. Ethical education in general for Aristotle is the process of improving perception or discernment by modifying desire and imparting true beliefs.

24 C. Mallory, "Acts of Objectification and the Repudiation of Dominance: Leopold, Ecofeminism, and the Ecological Narrative," *Ethics & the Environment* 6, no. 2 (2001): 59-89. Mallory, intentionally or not, misrepresents Leopold's position so that this childish trophy collection becomes the whole point of hunting for Leopold!

25 M. C. Nussbaum, "The Discernment of Perception: An Aristotelian Conception of Private and Public Rationality." This last requirement of educated discernment bears emphasis because another name for this is practical wisdom or prudence in Aristotelian terms.

PART THREE

Chapter Seven

1 It is important to note that these various activities are in no way actual competitors: one can and, I think, one should practice as many of them as one can find the time for. When, for example one both gardens and practices field sports, one becomes quickly aware of the differences and similarities. Indeed, this is the direction advocates of eating local foods should take.

2 Indeed, at a conference where I presented some of these ideas, a member of the audience suggested I just pull carrots instead of hunting or fishing!

3 Jensen, "The Virtues of Hunting."

4 Pollan, *The Omnivore's Dilemma: A Natural History of Four Meals.* For Pollan, a crucial difference between gardening and hunting is the heightened perceptual awareness he experiences while hunting. His senses are all on high alert. I shall discuss this feature as a difference in aesthetic competence, which results from frequently having this kind of experience.

5 Valdene, *For a Handful of Feathers.*

6 Michael Pollan, *Second Nature: A Gardener's Education* (New York: Grove Press, 1991), 124.

7 Ibid., 129.

8   Martha C. Nussbaum, "Non-Relative Virtues," in *Moral Relativism: A Reader*, ed. Paul K. Moser and Thomas L. Carson (New York: Oxford University Press, 2002), 202. " . . . we can understand progress in ethics, like progress in scientific understanding, to be progress in finding the correct, fuller specification of a virtue, isolated by its thin or nominal definition. This progress is aided by a perspicuous mapping of the sphere of grounding experiences." 205.

9   I don't advocate for a strict distinction between "wildness" and "culture" because there are so many examples of overlap: stocked fish, farm-raised pheasants, and deer control garden fencing come to mind.

10   A. Leopold, *A Sand County Almanac with Essays on Conservation from Round River*. 223-24.

11   My birddog fails to make this distinction. For her, the garden is a place to point insects and the woods are a place to point birds.

12   See Kerasote's discussion of this in Ted Kerasote, *Bloodties: Nature, Culture, and the Hunt* (New York: Random House, 1993).

13   Jensen, "The Virtues of Hunting." 121.

14   J. Ortega y Gasset, *Meditations on Hunting* (Bozeman, MT: Wilderness Adventure Press, 1995). 103-4.

15   Sherman, "The Habituation of Character." " . . . emotions cannot be shaped without some simultaneous cultivation of discriminatory abilities. This is included as a part of habituation." 243.

16   Jensen, "The Virtues of Hunting." 122.

17   Ibid., 118, 119.

18   Matthew Brower, *Developing Animals: Wildlife and Early American Photography* (Minneapolis: University of Minnesota Press, 2011).

Chapter Eight

1   Mallory, "Acts of Objectification and the Repudiation of Dominance: Leopold, Ecofeminism, and the Ecological Narrative," 109.

2   See for example Martha C. Nussbaum, *Frontiers of Justice: Disability, Nationality, Species Membership*. She says her view implies "a ban on hunting and fishing for sport, which inflict painful deaths on animals." 396. Nearly every critic seems to feel the need to say that it is only *sport* hunting or fishing they are condemning. See also Mallory, "Acts of Objectification and the Repudiation of Dominance: Leopold, Ecofeminism, and the Ecological Narrative." She says, "Sport hunting is an inherently oppressive act." 68

3   P. V. Moriarty and M. Woods, "Hunting [Is Not Identical to] Predation," *Environmental Ethics* 19 (1997): 391-404. "From this brief outline of the history of hunting in the United States, we see that wild animals have been regarded as either commodities, recreational resources, or nuisances. Not only will Western culture continue to thrive in the U.S. with or without hunting, but the cultural history of hunting provides no moral justification for the continued practice of hunting today." 403.

4   S. R. Kellert, "Attitudes and Characteristics of Hunters and Anti-hunters and Related Policy Suggestions," in *Transactions of the North American Wildlife and Natural Resources Conference*, 1978.

5   P. S. Wenz, "Environmental Activism and Appropriate Monism," in *Environmental Philosophy and Environmental Activism* (Lanham, Maryland: Rowman & Littlefield Publishers, 1995), 215-27. Wenz says there is no contradiction in condemning sport hunting and allowing subsistence hunting so long as there are "relevant differences of sufficient evaluative weight to justify distinguishing" the two. 217. I shall argue that there are no such relevant differences.

6   R. Caras, *Death as a Way of Life* (Boston: Little Brown and Co., 1970). 126, my emphasis.

7   Of course there are some people who hunt to kill. At least, they say this and likely mean it. But then there are also people who eat to overcome boredom but that does not make this the goal of eating as a practice. People may participate in an activity for their own idiosyncratic reasons but the defining goals of the activity itself remain independent.

8   See for an example of this Ted Kerasote, *Bloodties: Nature, Culture, and the Hunt*, 115. See also David Petersen, *Heartsblood: Hunting, Spirituality, and Wildness in America* (Washington, D.C.: Island Press/Shearwater Books, 2000).

9   Theodore Vitali, "Sport Hunting: Moral or Immoral?" *Environmental Ethics* 12 (1990): 77.

10 Matt Cartmill, *A View to a Death in the Morning: Hunting and Nature through History* (Cambridge: Harvard University Press, 1993). See Chapter 8 for discussion of misanthropy and hunting.

11 G. L. Comstock, "Subsistence Hunting," in *Food for Thought: The Debate over Eating Meat*, ed. S.F. Sapontzis (Amherst, NY: Prometheus Books, 2004), 306. See also Mallory, "Acts of Objectification and the Repudiation of Dominance: Leopold, Ecofeminism, and the Ecological Narrative," 65.

12 Comstock, "Subsistence Hunting." 306.

13 N. S. Momaday, "A First American's View," in *Environmental Ethics: Divergence and Convergence* (Boston: McGraw Hill, 1998), 252-56. Momaday describes a typical indigenous man of five hundred years ago in this way: "this latter-day man . . . is only incidentally a hunter; he is also a fisherman, a husbandman, even a physician. He fells trees and builds canoes; he grows corn, squash, and beans, and he gathers fruits and nuts. . . ." 253.

14 Kerasote, *Bloodties: Nature, Culture, and the Hunt*, 41.

15 See Paul Greenberg, *Four Fish: The Future of the Last Wild Food* (New York: The Penguin Press, 2010). Greenberg's experience fishing in Alaska with Yupik natives illustrates in fascinating detail the complexity of "subsistence fishing."

16 Stephen E. Ambrose. *Undaunted Courage* (New York: Touchstone, 1996).

17 J. D. Rabb, "The Vegetarian Fox and Indigenous Philosophy: Speciesism, Racism, and Sexism," *Environmental Ethics* 24, no. 3 (Fall 2002): 275-94. Rabb argues that this is a pernicious fallacy. He makes a compelling case that morally to exempt indigenous cultures by virtue of their "hunting for survival" is not just to oversimplify their cultures but to demean them as well.

18 Dunlap, *Saving America's Wildlife*; G. G. Gray, *Wildlife and People: The Human Dimension of Wildlife Ecology* (Chicago: University of Illinois Press, 1993); Reiger, *American Sportsmen and the Origins of Conservation*; Warren, *The Hunter's Game: Poachers and Conservationist in Twentieth-Century America*.

19 Len Olsen, "Contemplating the Intentions of Anglers: The Ethicist's Challenge," *Environmental Ethics* 25, no. 3 (2003): 267-77. He says " . . . the only thing that distinguishes . . . a case of sport fishing and . . . a case of sustenance fishing, is the intention of the fisherman." 276-77.

20 Wade, "Animal Liberationism, Ecocentrism, and the Morality of Sport Hunting." 16.

21 J. A. Cohan, "Is Hunting a 'Sport?'" *International Journal of Applied Philosophy* 17, no. 2 (2003): 291. Joy Williams derides sport hunting as: "A jolly game of mutual satisfaction between the hunter and the hunted—*Bam, bam, bam, I get to shoot you and you get to be dead.*" Joy Williams, "The Killing Game" in Pam Houston, ed., *Women on Hunting* (Hopewell, NJ: The Ecco Press, 1995), 252.

22 James A. Swan, *In Defense of Hunting* (San Francisco: Harper, 1995), 274.

23 Ted Kerasote, *Heart of Home: People, Wildlife, Place* (New York: Villard, 1997), 187. Holmes Rolston III, *Environmental Ethics: Duties to and Values in the Natural World* (Philadelphia: Temple University Press,1988), 91. See also David Petersen, *Heartsblood: Hunting, Spirituality, and Wildness In America* (Washington, D.C.: Island Press, 2000), 80.

24 Ortega y Gasset, *Meditations on Hunting*, 105. See also W. Wick, "The Rat and the Squirrel, or The Rewards of Virtue," *Ethics* 82, no. 1 (October 1971): 21-32. Wick makes the same point about sport fishing. In sport fishing, he says, ". . . ends and means change places— that is, the actual fish became a means of focusing and intensifying the activity instead of being the reason for it . . . the point was an exercise of powers and skill—something that can be achieved quite satisfactorily whether or not a creel or a boat gets filled with fish." 26.

25 See Marti Kheel, "The Killing Game: An Ecofeminist Critique of Hunting." *Journal of the Philosophy of Sport* 23 (1996): 30-44. Kheel details these and other reasons for excluding hunting from the category of sport.

26 Clair Powers and Francis O'Gorman, "Animals, Power and Ethics: The Case of Foxhunting," in *Moral and Political Reasoning in Environmental Practice* (Cambridge: MIT Press, 2003), 281-94. See also Cohan, "Is Hunting a 'Sport?'" He says fox hunting "has been pursued for the amusement, for the niceties of its English protocol, and for its social camaraderie." 297.

27 It is of some interest that one of the captains on "Most Dangerous Catch" recently made public his opposition to oil drilling in parts of Alaska. See also Greenberg, who in *Four Fish: The Future of the Last Wild Food*, argues that some commercial fishermen are starting to use environmental criteria.

28 A. A. Luce, *Fishing and Thinking* (Camden, Maine: Ragged Mountain Press, 1959), 179.

29 J. McPhee, *The Founding Fish* (New York: Farrar, Straus and Giroux, 2002), 325.

30 See for example the survey of opinions in T. Kerasote, "Catch and Deny," in *Heart of Home*, 107-22.

Chapter Nine

1   Some of the argument in this chapter is based upon C. List, "On the Moral Significance of a Hunting Ethic," *Ethics & the Environment* 3, no. 2 (1998): 157-75.

2   Sapontzis, *Morals, Reason, and Animals,* 266.

3   Kheel, "License to Kill: An Ecofeminist Critique of Hunter's Discourse," 87.

4   Ibid. 110.

5   On the issue of feminism and hunting see the excellent analysis in M. Z. Stange, *Woman the Hunter* (Boston: Beacon Press, 1997).

6   B. Luke, "A Critical Analysis of Hunter's Ethics," *Environmental Ethics* 19 (1997): 25-44.

7   See for example the "New York Sportsman" code of conduct for hunters at the "Official Site of the New York Sportsman," http://ny-sportsman.com/code_conduct.htm.

8   *Today's Hunter: A Guide to Hunting Responsibly and Safely,* 69-70.

9   I have been unable to find this quote in Leopold. However he does say something like it in several places.

10 A. Leopold, *A Sand County Almanac with Essays on Conservation from Round River,* 212. This is perhaps the source of the quote at the beginning of the Sportsman Code mentioned above.

11 J. Posewitz, *Beyond Fair Chase: The Ethic and Tradition of Hunting,* 57. See also Edward Hanna, "Fair Chase: To Where Does It Lead?" in *The Culture of Hunting in Canada,* ed. Jean L. Manore and Dale G. Miner (Vancouver: UBC Press, 2007), 239-61. Hanna presents a determined critique of this doctrine when it is interpreted as rules of fair play for a sport.

12 It is also important that this awareness is equated with "their management needs."

13 A. Leopold, *A Sand County Almanac with Essays on Conservation from Round River.* 190.

14 Jon Moline, "Aldo Leopold and the Moral Community," *Environmental Ethics* 8 (1986): 99-120.

15 For an interesting contrast see Sean Patrick Farrell, "The Urban Deerslayer," *The New York Times,* November 24, 2009. See also T. Kerasote, *Heart of Home.*

16 A. Leopold, *A Sand County Almanac with Essays on Conservation from Round River.* 293.

PART FOUR

Chapter Ten

1   Wensveen says: "In order to ensure ecosystem sustainability we will often have to enhance or change certain social conditions and economic patterns. The need for such enhancements and changes points to the wider goal of a sustainable society, a goal that shows promise as a social vision, but the has not yet been linked systematically to virtue ethics." Wensveen. "Ecosystem Sustainability as a Criterion for Genuine Virtue, " 240.

2   Swanson, *The Public and the Private in Aristotle's Political Philosophy*, 10.

3   A. Leopold, *A Sand County Almanac with Essays on Conservation from Round River.* 211, my emphasis.

4   J. E. Dizard, *Mortal Stakes: Hunters and Hunting in Contemporary America* (Amherst: University of Massachusetts Press, 2003), chap. seven. Dizard is clearly concerned with the same forces under discussion here.

5   A. Leopold, "The Outlook for Farm Wildlife," in *For the Health of the Land* (Washington, D.C.: Island Press, 1999), 218.

6   Aristotle, *Politics*, bk. I, chap. 8, 1256b27-31.

7   Ibid. 1257b38-1258a3. Worster argues that the concept of ecology is historically related to that of household management and economics as found in Aristotle. D. Worster, *Nature's Economy: The Roots of Ecology* (Garden City, NY: Anchor Books, 1979).

8   See Swanson. *The Public and the Private in Aristotle's Political Philosophy*, 135.

9   Aristotle, *Politics*, bk. VII, chap. 14, 1333a30-b3. See also John O'Neill. *Ecology, Policy and Politics: Human Well-Being and the Natural World.* 170-71.

10 Richard Louv, *Last Child in the Woods: Saving Our Children from Nature-Deficit Disorder* (Chapel Hill: Algonquin Books of Chapel Hill, 2008). Ironically, Louv is unwilling to endorse hunting as a way to overcome this deficit.

11 Pollan, *Second Nature: A Gardener's Education.*

12 Susan Flader, "Building Conservation on the Land: Aldo Leopold and the Tensions of Professionalism and Citizenship," in *Reconstructing Conservation: Finding Common Ground*, ed. Ben Minteer and Robert Manning (Washington, D. C.: Island Press, 2003), 115-32. "It is [the tradition of civic organizing] out of which much of our American conservation movement grew, including Leopold's efforts to organize game protective associations. . . ." 120.

13 O'Neill, *Ecology, Policy and Politics: Human Well-Being and the Natural World*, 162.

Chapter Eleven

1   Jim Posewitz, *Inherit the Hunt: A Journey into the Heart of American Hunting* (Guilford, Connecticut: Falcon, 1999), 104.

2   Ibid., 106.

3   Ibid., 108.

4   A. Leopold, *A Sand County Almanac with Essays on Conservation from Round River*, 216.

5   S. Pohl, "Technology and the Wilderness Experience," *Environmental Ethics* 28, no. 2 (2006): 149.

6   Pohl doesn't see the tight connection between excellence in outdoor recreation and environmental virtues. She relies on a rather standard list of virtues.

7   Pohl, "Technology and the Wilderness Experience," 154. She derives this distinction from Albert Borgmann, *Technology and the Character of Contemporary Life* (Chicago: University of Chicago Press, 1984).

8   J. L. Hemingway, "Leisure and Democracy: Incompatible Ideals?" in *Leisure and Ethics: Reflections on the Philosophy of Leisure* (Reston, VA: American Alliance for Health, Physical Education, Recreation and Dance, 1991), 77.

9   See for instance the criticism of Trout Unlimited in William Washabaugh and Catherine Washabaugh, *Deep Trout: Angling in Popular Culture* (New York: Berg, 2000).

Chapter Twelve

1   Note that this is broader than the education for beginning hunters and anglers. For Aristotle, education is necessary for the development of practical wisdom; it's a life-long commitment. See Swanson, 160.

2   There are very few states that do anything at all about angler education. See Bruce Matthews and Cheryl Riley, *Teaching and Evaluating Outdoor Ethics Education Programs* (National Wildlife Federation, 1995).

3   C. Lord, *Education and Culture in the Political Thought of Aristotle* (Ithaca: Cornell University Press, 1982), 36.

4   *Today's Hunter: A Guide to Hunting Responsibly and Safely*, 4. IHEA and others involved in hunter education might refrain from promising to cultivate the big name virtues of honesty, self-discipline, self-reliance,

etc. We, of course, hope these aspects of character are developed at some point by everyone, but, as I've argued, it is not at all clear that this classical version of the sportsman thesis is defensible. What is defensible is the claim that field sports develop *environmental* virtues. Also, compare this problem with that faced by public schools charged with character education.

5   Ibid., 72.

6   Louv, *Last Child in the Woods: Saving Our Children from Nature-Deficit Disorder.*

7   *Today's Hunter: A Guide to Hunting Responsibly and Safely*, 47.

8   Ibid., 88.

Chapter Thirteen

1   Cartmill, *A View to a Death in the Morning: Hunting and Nature Through History*, chap. three.

2   Reiger, *American Sportsmen and the Origins of Conservation*; Dunlap, *Saving America's Wildlife*. See also J. A. Tober, *Who Owns the Wildlife?* (Westport, CN: Greenwood Press, 1981).

3   Dunlap, *Saving America's Wildlife*, 13.

4   Ortega y Gasset, *Meditations on Hunting*, 128.

5   H. Dahles, "Game Killing and Killing Games: An Anthropologist Looking at Hunting in a Modern Society," *Society and Animals* 1, no. 2 (1993): 179.

6   Ibid.

7   For instance, the attitudes of sportsmen were a crucial factor in support of the predator extermination policies pursued in the early twentieth century. Fox, *The American Conservation Movement: John Muir and His Legacy*, chap. five.

8   J. A. Pauley, "The Value of Hunting," *Journal of Value Inquiry* 37, no. 2 (2003): 233-44.

9   Cartmill, *A View to a Death in the Morning: Hunting and Nature Through History*, 29. Cartmill says game animals are considered "wild" because they are "not friendly toward people or submissive to their authority. . . ." This preposterous definition might work for "wild" teenagers, but not animals.

10   A. Leopold, *A Sand County Almanac with Essays on Conservation from Round River*, 146.

11   Aldo Leopold, *Game Management.*, p. 394. Pheasants were not high on Leopold's list of game because they are non-native and might, he thought, displace native species.

12   For a compelling discussion, see David Baron, *The Beast in the Garden* (New York: W. W. Norton & Company, 2004).

13   See R. Scruton, "Ethics and Welfare: The Case of Hunting," *Philosophy: the Journal of the British Institute of Philosophical Studies* 77 (October 2002): 543-64. Scruton argues that justified hunting must take into account the evolved behavior of animals, especially those ways the animals are threatened by predators. So he gives an argument against snaring, poisoning, and shining because hunting "simulates a form of predation with which—arguably at least—the quarry is by nature able to deal." 564.

Chapter Fourteen

1   See for instance P. Cafaro, "Gluttony, Arrogance, Greed, and Apathy: An Exploration of Environmental Vice," in *Environmental Virtue Ethics* (Lanham: Rowman & Littlefield Publishers, 2005), 146.

2   One of the most thoroughly documented outdoor activities is fly fishing. Why fly fishing attracts historians, sociologists, and philosophers may be due to its "contemplative" reputation. Regardless of the reason, as Sax notes, there are thousands of books on fly fishing and a good number of them are not "how to" but concerned with history, philosophy, and cultural issues generally.

3   Joseph Sax, *Mountains Without Handrails: Reflection on the National Parks* (Ann Arbor: University of Michigan Press, 1980), 45.

4   Ibid., 29.

Chapter Fifteen

1   Kerasote, *Heart of Home*, 182-83.

INDEX

catch-and-release fishing, 80–81, 110

character, 27, 31, 88

character development, 9, 16, 24, 32, 76, 107, 114–16

cheating. *See* skill shortcuts

civic engagement, 104–6, 112

civic virtues, 31, 32–33, 98–106, 110

class distinctions, 19, 38, 70, 75, 80, 120

codes for field sports. *See* sporting codes

codes for fish and game, 121

commercial hunting and angling, 19, 39, 80

commercialism, force of, 10, 97, 109–11

community, biotic. *See* biotic community

community of practitioners, 32

companionship, 17, 32

competitions, 79–80, 96–97, 110–11

competitive sports, 76, 78

Compleat Angler, The (Walton), 15

connectedness, 68

conservation
 interest groups, 96, 104–5
 as means to preserve game species, 38, 39–40
 support for as character standard for sportsmen, 25
 as a tenet of sporting codes, 93, 95

"Conservation Esthetic" (Leopold), 58, 82

conservation practices, 43, 47, 50, 80, 105

consumerism, 105

contemplation, virtue of, 15–16, 25

contemplative recreation, 130

courage, virtue of, 14–16, 25

crab fishing, 80

Crawford, Matthew, 26

criticism of field sports. *See* field sports, criticism of

cultural value, 74–75, 100, 108

cycle of life, 62

Czech-style nymphing, 23

Dahles, Heidi, 121

dependence on nature, 68, 100

Dersu the Trapper (Arseniev), 54

destination hunting and fishing, 107, 109–10, 111–12

devices. *See* gadgets

diversity of the biotic community, 43, 44, 45–46, 124

dogs, 24, 108–9

domestic settings and communities, 62, 64

ecological conscience, virtue of, 37, 49, 50–53, 66, 102
 See also environmental virtues

ecology
 of biotic communities, 40, 58, 128
 ignorance of, 91
 learned by nature study, 49, 55–56, 57, 91
 teaching of, 55, 118–19

economic value
 of the biotic community, 44
 in environmental decision-making, 50, 101, 135
 as primary value, 107, 110

education
 formal schooling, 21, 55, 57
 programs for sportsmen, 17, 85, 97, 113–19
 technical *vs.* moral, 18, 27, 91, 113–15
 of youth (*See* youth, education of)

elitism, 19, 70–71, 110

emotional response, 49, 56–57, 58, 67–68

environmental awareness, virtue of, 37, 49, 53, 54, 59, 66

See also environmental virtues

environmental decision-making, 50

environmental ethics, 36–37

environmental knowledge, 54, 59, 91, 123

environmental organizations, 96, 104–5

environmental virtues, 36–37, 48, 66, 136

and sporting codes, 87–95

ethical categories, 70, 72–73

ethical judgment, 32, 50, 80

evolution, 44, 53, 56, 57
  learned by nature study, 91
  process of, 123, 125
  teaching of, 118–19

excellence, pursuit of, 27, 29, 30, 47–48, 118

expertise, 21, 23, 24, 25, 27, 33, 63

factory farms, 92, 103

fair chase, 9, 52, 86, 89–90

falconry, 132

farming, 51, 101–2, 127

field sports, criticism of
  and animal rights and welfare, 12, 18, 60–61, 66, 71–72, 81, 98
  class-based, 19, 70–71
  and fair chase, 89
  feminist, 84
  as promoting vice, 18

field sports, future of, 10, 12, 94, 100–101, 106–7

field sports, participatory nature of, 56–57, 67

field sports, privatization of, 110

field sports, substitutions for. See gardening; wildlife photography

field sports, ultimate requirement of, 67, 68

field sports and character development. See character development

fighting spirit, animals with, 120–22

firearms
  safety education for, 113, 115–17
  as source of conflict, 116, 135

as tools for hunting, 86, 107, 108, 117

fish finders, 52, 90, 111

flow, 57, 64

fly fishing, 23–24, 33, 131, 133

fly-tying, 24, 117

food
  as connection to the biotic community, 62, 87, 119, 125, 129
  as justification for field sports, 81
  locally-derived, 62, 92–93, 102–3
  preparation of, 105, 119

food chains
  awareness of, 45, 58, 62, 100
  and the biotic good, 43, 44
  disconnection from, 101, 104
  and field sports, 56, 64, 125
  responsibility for, 92, 93

forestry, 51

fox hunting, 15, 80

gadgets, 107–9
  See also technology, hunting and angling

game animals
  beauty of, 93, 122, 123–24
  character traits of, 120–22, 123–24
  definitions of, 119–22
  populations of, 38–40, 118, 120, 122, 126
  stocked, 26, 42, 52, 120, 122, 124–27
  wild, 124–26

game calling, 117

Game Management (Leopold), 128

gardening, 61–66, 132

gentlemanliness
  characteristics of, 35, 89, 120
  as goal of field sports, 17, 25, 38, 39, 70

good of the biotic community
  See biotic good

the good, 36
the good life, 36, 99, 102, 105
government involvement in
    conservation, 40
    See also policies, state and federal
GPS (global positioning system), 108
Greenlanders, 73, 74
guns. *See* firearms

habits, 27, 29, 31, 114, 115
habituation
    See practice
happiness, 20, 29, 31, 36, 102
Hemingway, J.L., 112
Homiak, Marcia, 32
humans, 46, 50, 53, 58, 64, 121, 124
humility, 68, 91
hunches, 25–26
hunter education courses, 17, 85, 97,
    113–19
hunting
    contrasted with angling, 15–16
    definition of, 16, 71–73
hunting and fishing, categories
    of. *See* commercial; sport;
    subsistence
hunting and gathering, 73–75, 132
hunting licenses, 113, 117
husbandry, 87, 93–95, 104–5, 112,
    117, 132

ice fishing, 74
imported game animals. *See* non-
    native species
indigenous peoples, 70, 74
industrial food production, 92, 103
Inherit the Hunt (Posewitz), 106
injury as a risk of hunting, 15–16
insect collecting, 131
insects, 65
instructors
    See teachers; mentors
integrity of the biotic community,
    42, 43–44

intellectual virtues, 28, 31, 32, 53
interests, 32, 54, 55
International Hunter Education
    Association (IHEA), 114
intuitive knowledge, 54–55, 63–64
invasive species
    See non-native species

Jensen, Jon, 62, 67–68
judgment, ethical, 32, 50, 80
justification for field sports
    ecological, 118
    economic, 107
    moral, 10, 62, 74
    obtaining food, 81

kayaking, 129, 133, 135
Kerasote, Ted, 74, 77, 137
killing animals, 61, 62, 67–68, 70,
    71, 77
    as immoral behavior, 84
knowledge
    background, 22, 23, 47, 59, 64
    environmental, 54, 59, 91, 123
    intuitive, 63–64
    scientific, 32, 49, 54, 55, 63, 123,
        126

land, carrying capacity of, 118
land aesthetics. *See* biotic community
land ethic, 37, 41, 42–46, 87, 131
land mechanism, 45, 53–54, 91
land pyramid, 45, 49, 53
land use, 101, 112
the *Laws* (Plato), 14
learning processes, 21
leisure activities, 27, 29–33, 99, 112
Leopold, Aldo
    on aesthetic competence, 56–58,
        65
    on ecology, 91, 124, 128
    on ethical behavior, 10, 86, 88
    and the land ethic, 42–45

Peck, John Mason, 39

perception, 33–34, 49, 56–58, 65
    See also biotic perception

photography, 61, 66–69, 132

phronesis
    See practical reason

Pinchot, Gifford, 38

Piscator the angler, 15

place-based memories, 68

plant collecting, 131

Plato, 14, 25, 119

pleasure, 29

Pohl, Sarah, 108

policies, state and federal
    to maintain game populations,
        39–40, 81, 118
    for predator control, 42, 91
    for stocking game animals, 42, 96,
        125–27

political action, 104–5

the *Politics* (Aristotle), 102

Pollan, Michael, 62, 63, 103

Posewitz, Jim, 89, 106, 109

pot hunters. *See* commercial hunting
    and angling

practical reason
    and expertise, 22–24, 33, 35
    and field sports, 26–27, 51, 59
    gardening as an activity of, 62, 63
    as precondition for virtue
        formation, 31, 47, 53
    as problem-solving, 22–23

practice (habituation), 21, 22, 24,
    27–28, 76, 114

practices of conservation, 43, 47, 50,
    80, 105

practitioners, community of, 32

predators
    elimination of, 51, 91, 127–28
    as part of the biotic community,
        43, 45, 126

private lands, 40, 41, 96, 112

privilege, 70–71

prizes for hunting and fishing,
    79–80, 81, 97, 110–11

problem solving, 22–23, 27
    See also practical reason

problems with the sportsman thesis,
    18–19, 60–70

production, arts of, 64

professionalization of field sports, 96,
    110–11

public access to field sports, 94,
    106–7, 110, 112

public image of field sports, 87, 98,
    106, 118

quarry. *See* game animals

racism, 19, 70, 75

Rawls, John, 31

reasons for hunting and angling, 74,
    75, 79, 128–29

recreation, outdoor. *See* outdoor
    recreation

regulations
    for fishing, 81
    as means of conservation, 38–40
    necessary for survival of field
        sports, 94

relevance of field sports, 50

restraint, virtue of
    challenges to, 52, 88
    as characteristic of sportsmen,
        39, 90
    in economic matters, 101, 105

rise forms, 24, 65

rock climbing, 77, 131, 133, 134–35

Rolston, Holmes, 77

Roochnik, David, 18

Roosevelt, Theodore, 9, 17, 19, 34,
    38, 39, 40

Ruffed Grouse Society, 105

rules
    as necessary for beginners, 22–23,
        26, 83, 90
    self-imposed, 89
    and sporting codes, 84–90

Rush, Dr. Benjamin, 18

tools of hunting and angling, 107–9, 133

tournaments, 79–80, 96–97, 110–11

traditions, 25, 73–74, 81, 100, 103

training animals, 108–9, 131–32

trash fish, 122, 127–28

trophies, 17, 58

Trout Unlimited, 104

ultimate requirement of field sports, 67, 68

United States Fish and Wildlife Service, 118

vacations. *See* destination hunting and fishing

value. *See* cultural value; economic value; split-rail value

variables. *See* luck; stochastic arts

varmints, 127–28

Venator, the hunter, 15

vice, produced by field sports, 18

victory, 76–77

video games, 31–32, 99

virtue ethics, 36–38, 60

virtues
    defining the character of the sportsman, 9, 59
    definition of, 28
    development of, 20, 24, 29–32, 79–80
    generation of by field sports, 11, 16, 59, 82, 136
    See also civic virtues; environmental virtues; intellectual virtues; moral virtues

Vitali, Theodore, 72

Walton, Izaak, 15, 25, 102

war, hunting as training for, 14–15, 100

White, Stuart Edward, 39

wildlife-human conflicts, 107

"Wildlife in American Culture" (Leopold), 100

wildlife management
    and need for ecological conscience, 51–52
    role of field sports in, 10, 106–7, 114, 117–18
    state and federal policies for, 40, 42, 81, 91, 96, 118, 125–27

wildlife photography, 61, 66–69, **132**

wild settings and communities, 62–63, 64, 68, 124, 130

women, 70

work, 29

youth, education of
    by mentors, 9, 49, 115
    in school, 55
    and the sportsman thesis, 14
    for virtue development, 14, **29**, 31, 58, 117